Viber for Everyone

Messaging, Calling, and More Made Easy

Kiet Huynh

Table of Contents

Introduction..5

  1.1 Why Viber?...5

  1.2 What This Book Covers...10

  1.3 How to Use This Guide...15

PART I Getting Started with Viber 19

  2.1 What Is Viber?...19

  2.2 Setting Up Your Viber Account...23

  2.3 Navigating the Viber Interface...33

  2.4 Syncing Viber Across Devices 43

PART II Messaging and Calling Essentials..48

  3. Messaging Made Easy..48

    3.1 Sending and Receiving Messages...48

    3.2 Using Stickers and Emojis to Enhance Conversations...........................57

    3.3 Sending Photos, Videos, and Files 62

    3.4 Using Voice Messages 68

    3.5 Organizing Chats and Archiving Conversations.......................................73

  4. Calling with Viber..82

    4.1 Making Voice Calls...82

    4.2 Using Video Calls...87

    4.3 Group Calls: Stay Connected with Multiple People.................................91

    4.4 Call Quality Tips and Tricks 95

    4.5 Viber Out: Calling Non-Viber Users 99

PART III Advanced Viber Features...104

  5. Group Chats and Communities...104

    5.1 Creating and Managing Group Chats...104

5.2 Using Polls in Group Chats...109

5.3 Joining and Participating in Viber Communities..114

5.4 Customizing Group Chat Settings 119

6. Privacy and Security on Viber...**125**

6.1 Understanding Viber's Encryption and Privacy Features....................................125

6.2 Managing Who Can Contact You 129

6.3 Setting Up PIN Lock and Hidden Chats..134

6.4 Blocking and Reporting Unwanted Contacts 138

7. Customizing Your Viber Experience...**143**

7.1 Changing Themes and Chat Backgrounds...143

7.2 Customizing Notifications 147

7.3 Creating and Using Your Own Stickers...152

7.4 Personalizing Your Profile 156

8. Exploring Advanced Features...**162**

8.1 Using Viber on Desktop...162

8.2 Scheduling Messages..167

8.3 Managing Multiple Accounts..171

8.4 Setting Up Shortcuts and Quick Replies...175

8.5 Discovering Viber Bots and Services 179

PART IV Support and Safety..**183**

9. Troubleshooting and Support...**183**

9.1 Common Issues and How to Solve Them...183

9.2 Contacting Viber Support...188

9.3 Staying Updated with New Features 193

10. Staying Safe on Viber...**198**

10.1 Identifying and Avoiding Scams 198

10.2 Using Two-Step Verification...202

10.3 Maintaining Online Etiquette...206

Conclusion **211**

11.1 Why Viber is the Best Choice for Messaging and Calls 211

Appendices **216**

A. Viber Keyboard Shortcuts..216

B. Glossary of Common Viber Terms...220

Acknowledgments..232

Introduction

More than messaging

With a variety of calling and messaging features, you have endless options when it comes to expressing yourself

Voice and video calls

High-quality calls for a quick 'hello' or a much-needed face-to-face

Group chats & calls

Like and reply to messages in group chats or start a group video or voice call instantly

Stickers & GIFs

Endless stickers and GIFs for every possible expression. Not enough? Create your own

On mobile & desktop

Chats are 100% synced between devices including 1-tap transfer of calls

Discover More Features

1.1 Why Viber?

In an age where digital communication plays an essential role in our lives, choosing the right messaging app can feel overwhelming. Among the myriad of choices, **Viber** stands out as a versatile, user-friendly platform that has become a global favorite. Whether you want to stay connected with family, collaborate with colleagues, or engage with your favorite communities, Viber offers a seamless communication experience tailored to your needs. In this chapter, we'll explore the key reasons why Viber has become a top choice for millions of users around the world.

Global Reach and Accessibility

One of Viber's greatest strengths is its global accessibility. Available in over 190 countries, Viber connects people across borders without the traditional barriers of cost and infrastructure. Unlike SMS or phone calls, which often incur high charges when communicating internationally, Viber uses the internet to transmit messages and calls, allowing users to connect with anyone, anywhere, at little to no cost.

Moreover, Viber supports multiple languages, making it accessible to a diverse user base. Whether you speak English, Spanish, Arabic, or any of the other supported languages, Viber's localized interface ensures that the app is intuitive and easy to use.

Free and Affordable Communication

Cost-effectiveness is a critical factor for many users, and Viber delivers on this front. Sending text messages, sharing photos, or making voice and video calls is entirely free when both parties are using Viber. For users needing to contact non-Viber users, the **Viber Out** feature provides low-cost international calling rates, making it an excellent choice for individuals and businesses alike.

In comparison to traditional telecom services or even some competing apps, Viber's pricing model is hard to beat. This affordability is especially important for users in developing countries, where access to low-cost communication tools can significantly enhance connectivity.

High-Quality Voice and Video Calls

When it comes to call quality, Viber consistently receives high marks. Thanks to its advanced technology and robust infrastructure, Viber delivers crystal-clear voice and video calls, even in areas with limited internet connectivity. The app automatically adjusts call quality based on the strength of your internet connection, ensuring that you can communicate smoothly, whether you're on a high-speed Wi-Fi network or a slower mobile connection.

This feature has made Viber a preferred choice for personal and professional communication alike. Families can enjoy uninterrupted conversations across long distances, while businesses can rely on Viber for clear and reliable conference calls.

Privacy and Security

In today's digital age, privacy is more important than ever. Viber places a strong emphasis on user security, offering **end-to-end encryption** for all messages, calls, and shared files. This means that only you and your intended recipient can access the content of your communication, with no third party—including Viber—able to intercept or read your messages.

In addition to encryption, Viber provides features like **Hidden Chats**, which allow users to keep certain conversations private and locked behind a PIN. This focus on privacy makes Viber an excellent choice for individuals who value confidentiality and peace of mind.

Rich Messaging Features

Viber goes beyond basic texting, offering a host of features that make conversations more engaging and interactive. From sending **stickers** and **GIFs** to sharing photos, videos, and voice messages, Viber transforms ordinary chats into lively, multimedia experiences.

The app also allows users to create **polls** in group chats, making it easy to gather opinions or make group decisions. These features, combined with the ability to send files and documents, make Viber a versatile tool for both personal and professional use.

Group Chats and Communities

For those who enjoy group communication, Viber's **group chat** and **community** features are game-changers. Group chats allow users to connect with friends, family, or colleagues, while communities enable large-scale interactions around shared interests or hobbies.

Viber Communities can support an unlimited number of members, making them ideal for businesses, fan groups, or organizations looking to engage with a broad audience. With tools like polls, announcements, and pinned messages, community admins can effectively manage conversations and keep members informed.

Cross-Platform Compatibility

Viber's compatibility across multiple platforms is another reason for its widespread popularity. Whether you're using a smartphone, tablet, or desktop, Viber ensures a seamless experience across devices. The app automatically syncs your messages and calls, allowing you to switch between devices without missing a beat.

This cross-platform functionality is particularly valuable for users who rely on Viber for work, enabling them to stay connected and productive whether they're in the office or on the go.

Constant Innovation

Viber is not just a static app—it's constantly evolving to meet the needs of its users. The developers regularly introduce new features, such as **disappearing messages**, **chat extensions**, and **custom stickers**, ensuring that Viber remains relevant and competitive in the ever-changing landscape of communication tools.

This commitment to innovation keeps Viber fresh and exciting, offering users new ways to connect and express themselves.

Support for Businesses

Viber isn't just for personal use—it's also a powerful tool for businesses. The app's **Viber for Business** features allow companies to engage with customers through branded messaging, chatbots, and customer support channels. Businesses can also create communities to connect with their audience and share updates or promotions.

For small businesses, Viber provides an affordable and effective way to build customer relationships and enhance brand visibility.

Social Connection in a Digital Age

Finally, Viber excels at fostering social connection in an increasingly digital world. Whether you're reconnecting with a childhood friend, planning a family reunion, or staying in touch with coworkers, Viber makes communication simple, engaging, and meaningful.

Its combination of accessibility, features, and security ensures that users can focus on what matters most: building and maintaining relationships.

Conclusion

Choosing Viber is more than just selecting a messaging app—it's embracing a platform designed to connect people, enhance communication, and provide a secure and enjoyable user experience. With its global reach, rich features, and commitment to innovation, Viber has earned its place as one of the leading communication tools available today.

In the next section, we'll dive into the specifics of what this book covers and how it can help you make the most of Viber's incredible features.

1.2 What This Book Covers

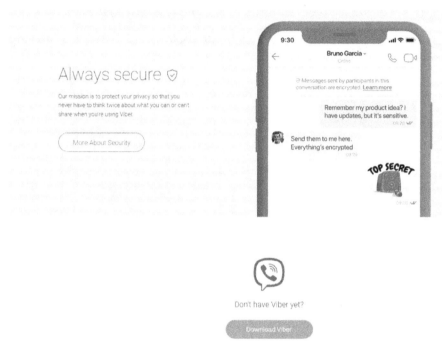

This book, **"Viber for Everyone: Messaging, Calling, and More Made Easy,"** is designed to be your comprehensive guide to mastering Viber, a versatile and user-friendly communication platform. Whether you are completely new to Viber or looking to maximize its features, this book provides a step-by-step roadmap to help you navigate, understand, and use the app effectively for personal and professional communication.

Let's break down exactly what this book covers to ensure you get the most out of it:

An Overview of Viber and Its Core Features

In the first part of the book, we delve into what Viber is and why it has become one of the most popular messaging and calling apps worldwide. We explore its history, its position in the market compared to other apps, and how it stands out in terms of security, simplicity, and cost-effectiveness.

You'll also learn about Viber's core features, including:

- Text messaging with emojis and stickers to make your conversations more expressive.

- Free voice and video calls for connecting with friends and family anywhere in the world.

- Group chats and communities that bring people together around shared interests or goals.

- File sharing, voice notes, and media sharing capabilities that make it easy to communicate in multiple ways.

- Viber Out, an affordable option to call non-Viber users on mobile or landline numbers.

This section ensures you understand the basics of Viber and sets the stage for you to explore its more advanced features later in the book.

Getting Started with Viber

The second part of the book guides you through setting up your Viber account and customizing it to suit your needs. Whether you are using an Android device, iPhone, tablet, or desktop, this section offers step-by-step instructions for installation and account creation.

You'll learn how to:

- Set up your account using your mobile number.

- Sync your contacts and invite friends to join Viber.

- Navigate the app interface and access its main functions.

- Use Viber on multiple devices seamlessly.

This chapter ensures you are fully prepared to begin using Viber confidently.

Mastering Messaging and Chats

One of the most popular uses of Viber is for messaging. This book dedicates a full section to exploring the many ways you can communicate through text, whether it's a one-on-one conversation or a group chat.

You'll discover:

- How to send and receive messages, including text, photos, videos, and voice notes.

- How to enhance your chats with stickers, GIFs, and emojis.

- Organizing and managing your chats, including archiving, deleting, and pinning conversations.

- Tips for using features like quick replies, message scheduling, and shortcuts.

Additionally, this section covers creating group chats and managing them effectively, from setting roles and permissions to using polls and media sharing.

Making Calls with Viber

For those who prefer talking over typing, Viber's voice and video call features are indispensable. This book provides detailed guidance on how to make the most of these features, including:

- Setting up and making one-on-one or group voice calls.

- Initiating high-quality video calls.

- Troubleshooting common call quality issues.

- Using the "Viber Out" feature to make affordable calls to non-Viber users.

You'll also learn how to switch between voice and video calls seamlessly and how to record calls when needed (if applicable in your region).

Privacy and Security Features

Privacy is a major concern in today's digital world, and Viber takes it seriously. This section of the book explains how Viber's end-to-end encryption works and what steps you can take to protect your account.

Topics include:

- Setting up two-step verification for added security.

- Understanding and managing the app's privacy settings.

- Blocking and reporting unwanted contacts or spam.

- Using hidden chats and PIN locks to keep sensitive conversations private.

With this knowledge, you'll be able to use Viber confidently, knowing your information is safe and secure.

Exploring Advanced Features

Beyond the basics, Viber offers many advanced features that can take your experience to the next level. This book walks you through:

- Setting up and managing Viber Communities.

- Using Viber on your desktop or laptop.

- Scheduling messages for future delivery.

- Creating and using custom stickers.

- Exploring Viber bots and services for entertainment, productivity, and shopping.

These advanced tools are designed to enhance your productivity and make Viber an even more enjoyable app to use.

Customizing Your Viber Experience

Every user has unique preferences, and Viber allows you to personalize your experience in several ways. This book covers:

- Changing themes and chat backgrounds.

- Customizing notifications to suit your lifestyle.

- Updating your profile picture and personal information.

By the end of this section, you'll know how to make Viber truly your own.

Troubleshooting and Support

Technology isn't always perfect, and issues can arise. This book equips you with the tools to troubleshoot common problems and access Viber's customer support when necessary.

You'll find answers to questions like:

- Why can't I connect to Viber?

- How do I recover a lost account?

- What should I do if my messages aren't sending?

This section ensures that you have the resources to solve problems quickly and effectively.

Tips for Power Users

For those who want to become Viber experts, this book offers tips and tricks to unlock the app's full potential. Topics include:

- Using Viber efficiently for work communication.

- Managing large communities with advanced admin tools.

- Exploring hidden features that many users overlook.

Whether you're a casual user or a power user, these tips will help you get the most out of Viber.

Staying Safe on Viber

Finally, this book emphasizes the importance of online safety. You'll learn how to identify and avoid scams, maintain good online etiquette, and ensure that your Viber experience is both safe and enjoyable.

1.3 How to Use This Guide

Welcome to the final section of the introduction, where we'll help you navigate this guide and make the most of its contents. Whether you're completely new to Viber or have been using it for a while but want to explore advanced features, this guide is structured to serve as a step-by-step roadmap for improving your Viber experience.

Understand the Layout

This book is divided into clear sections, each focusing on a specific aspect of Viber. Here's how it's organized:

1. **Introduction**: Provides a foundation for why Viber is an excellent choice, what the book covers, and who can benefit from it.

2. **Getting Started**: Helps you set up your Viber account, understand the interface, and sync your devices.

3. **Messaging and Calling Essentials**: Focuses on the core functionalities of Viber, including sending messages, making calls, and sharing files.

4. **Advanced Features**: Explores group chats, communities, privacy settings, and customization options.

5. **Support and Safety**: Offers guidance on troubleshooting, maintaining security, and staying safe online.

6. **Conclusion and Appendices**: Wraps up the book with key takeaways, advanced tips, and helpful resources.

Each chapter builds upon the previous one, making it easy for you to progress from beginner to advanced user at your own pace.

Who Can Use This Guide?

This guide is intentionally flexible and designed for a wide range of users. Whether you're:

- **A Complete Beginner**: You can start from the first chapter and follow the instructions step by step. The guide assumes no prior knowledge of Viber.

- **An Intermediate User**: If you're familiar with the basics, feel free to skip to the advanced features or troubleshooting sections.

- **An Advanced User**: Even seasoned users may discover new tricks and advanced features that improve productivity.

Think of this book as a reference you can return to anytime you have questions or want to learn something new.

How to Follow the Instructions

This guide uses a combination of step-by-step instructions, visual aids, and practical examples to make learning easy. Here's how to get the most out of it:

1. **Follow Step-by-Step Instructions**: Each section contains detailed, numbered steps for setting up and using features. For example, if you're learning how to make a group call, the steps are broken down into simple actions.

2. **Look for Visual Guides**: Where applicable, illustrations or descriptions of the interface are included to help you identify buttons, menus, and options.

3. **Try It Yourself**: After reading about a feature, try it on your own Viber app. This hands-on practice will reinforce what you've learned.

4. **Use the Tips and Tricks**: Throughout the book, you'll find highlighted boxes with useful tips, shortcuts, and advice for maximizing efficiency.

Adapting the Guide to Your Needs

Everyone uses Viber differently, and this guide is written with that flexibility in mind. Here are a few ways you can adapt it to your personal use:

- **Focus on Your Priorities**: If you primarily use Viber for messaging, concentrate on the chapters about texting, emojis, and file sharing. If calls are more important, explore the calling features in depth.

- **Skip and Refer Back**: Don't feel pressured to read every chapter in order. You can skip directly to sections that address your immediate questions and return later for more general learning.

- **Explore Advanced Features Gradually**: If you're new to Viber, focus on mastering the basics first. Once you're comfortable, move on to chapters about customization and advanced tools.

Icons and Symbols in the Guide

To make the guide more user-friendly, we've included the following symbols to highlight important information:

- 💡 **Tips**: Useful advice to save time and improve your experience.

- ⚠️ **Warnings**: Alerts about common pitfalls or issues to avoid.

- 📖 **Examples**: Real-life scenarios demonstrating how to use features effectively.

- 💡 **Key Points**: Important takeaways at the end of each section.

Keep an eye out for these icons as you read through the book. They'll help you quickly identify valuable insights.

Using This Guide Across Devices

Since Viber is available on both mobile and desktop platforms, this guide covers features for all devices. Here's how to approach it:

- **Mobile Users**: Focus on the chapters that explain the mobile interface and specific features optimized for smartphones.

- **Desktop Users**: Look for sections that cover desktop functionality, such as using Viber for work or managing accounts across devices.

- **Multi-Device Users**: Learn how to sync your chats and calls across your phone, tablet, and computer for a seamless experience.

Learn at Your Own Pace

This guide is designed for you to learn at a pace that suits you. Some readers may finish the book in one sitting, while others may prefer to read a chapter at a time and practice before moving on.

Here's a suggested approach:

1. Start with the **Introduction** to understand Viber's value and the guide's structure.

2. Follow the **Getting Started** section to set up your account and explore the basic interface.

3. Gradually move to **Messaging and Calling Essentials**, as these are the core features of Viber.

4. Dive into **Advanced Features** when you're ready to customize your experience.

5. Use the **Support and Safety** chapters whenever you need troubleshooting tips or want to ensure your account's security.

A Lifelong Reference

Finally, remember that this guide isn't just for learning—it's a resource you can return to whenever you need help. Whether it's troubleshooting a technical issue, discovering a hidden feature, or learning how to join a Viber Community, this book is your go-to manual.

Keep it handy, bookmark sections you find particularly useful, and don't hesitate to revisit it as Viber updates and adds new features over time.

By understanding how to use this guide, you're already taking the first step toward becoming a Viber pro. In the chapters that follow, we'll dive deeper into the app's features, show you how to master messaging and calling, and introduce you to the countless possibilities Viber offers. Let's get started!

PART I
Getting Started with Viber

2.1 What Is Viber?

In today's digitally connected world, communication apps have become a fundamental part of how we interact with friends, family, and colleagues. Among the numerous messaging apps available, **Viber** stands out as a versatile, feature-rich platform designed to cater to the needs of personal and professional communication. This chapter explores what Viber is, its history, core features, and how it has evolved into a powerful communication tool.

A Brief History of Viber

Viber was first launched in **2010** by four Israeli developers who sought to create a reliable and free alternative to traditional phone calls and SMS. Initially, Viber focused on providing high-quality voice calls over the internet (VoIP), competing with services like Skype. Over the years, it expanded to include messaging, video calls, group chats, and various other features.

In **2014**, Viber was acquired by Rakuten, a leading Japanese e-commerce and internet services company. Under Rakuten's ownership, Viber grew exponentially, integrating advanced features like end-to-end encryption, chatbots, and global business communication solutions.

Today, Viber has over **1 billion users worldwide**, making it one of the most popular messaging apps globally, especially in regions like Eastern Europe, the Middle East, and Asia.

Key Features of Viber

Viber sets itself apart from competitors like WhatsApp, Telegram, and Facebook Messenger through its comprehensive suite of features. Let's break down some of its core functionalities:

1. **Free Messaging and Calls**: Viber allows users to send unlimited text messages, photos, and videos for free, as long as they have an internet connection. Additionally, voice and video calls are also free when made to other Viber users.

2. **End-to-End Encryption**: Privacy and security are major selling points for Viber. All communications on the app are encrypted end-to-end, meaning only the sender and recipient can access the content of messages and calls.

3. **Viber Out**: Viber Out is a unique feature that enables users to make affordable international calls to non-Viber numbers, including landlines and mobile phones. This is particularly useful for travelers or individuals with family abroad.

4. **Stickers and Emojis**: Viber was one of the pioneers of introducing stickers to enhance conversations. Users can choose from thousands of fun, animated stickers to express themselves creatively.

5. **Group Chats and Communities**: Viber supports group chats with up to **250 participants**, making it ideal for families, friends, or small teams. Additionally, the Communities feature allows unlimited members, enabling users to create public or private spaces for shared interests.

6. **Cross-Platform Compatibility**: Viber is available on multiple platforms, including iOS, Android, Windows, macOS, and even Linux. This makes it easy to stay connected across all your devices.

7. **Customizable Experience**: Users can personalize their Viber experience by changing themes, customizing chat backgrounds, and creating their own stickers.

8. **Chat Extensions and Bots**: Viber supports interactive chat extensions, such as GIFs, YouTube, and music integrations. Additionally, businesses can use Viber chatbots to engage with customers.

Why Choose Viber Over Other Apps?

With so many messaging apps available, what makes Viber stand out? Here are some compelling reasons:

1. **Global Reach with Local Adaptation**: Viber's strength lies in its ability to cater to local needs. For example, Viber frequently partners with local businesses and governments to offer region-specific services.

2. **Focus on Security**: Unlike some competitors, Viber emphasizes privacy with its **Hidden Chats**, self-destructing messages, and the option to set PIN locks for sensitive conversations.

3. **Affordable International Communication**: Viber Out provides cost-effective calling rates to over 200 countries, making it an excellent choice for international communication.

4. **No Ads in Private Chats**: While some apps bombard users with ads, Viber keeps its private chats ad-free, ensuring a seamless communication experience.

How Viber Enhances Personal Communication

Viber is designed to bring people closer together. Whether it's a simple text, a heartfelt video call, or sharing photos from your latest vacation, Viber makes it easy to stay connected. Features like stickers, GIFs, and group chats add a touch of fun to everyday conversations.

How Viber Supports Businesses

In addition to personal communication, Viber has become a valuable tool for businesses. Companies use Viber to:

- Send marketing messages and promotions through broadcast lists.

- Create communities to engage with their customers.

- Provide customer support via chatbots and instant messaging.

For businesses looking for a professional edge, Viber offers the **Viber Business API**, which integrates seamlessly with CRM systems to streamline customer interactions.

The Future of Viber

As technology continues to evolve, Viber is constantly innovating to meet the demands of its users. Features like augmented reality (AR) filters, AI-powered chatbots, and advanced analytics for businesses are just a glimpse of what's to come.

Summary

Viber is more than just a messaging app; it's a versatile platform that simplifies communication while prioritizing privacy and security. Whether you're a casual user looking to stay in touch with loved ones or a business professional seeking new ways to engage customers, Viber has something for everyone.

By understanding what Viber is and what it offers, you're taking the first step toward mastering this powerful communication tool. In the next section, we'll guide you through setting up your Viber account and getting started with its basic features.

2.2 Setting Up Your Viber Account

Setting up your Viber account is the first step in unlocking the app's potential for seamless communication. This chapter will guide you through the process, from downloading and installing the app to customizing your profile for a personal touch. Whether you're a beginner or transitioning from another messaging platform, this section will ensure you have a smooth start.

Downloading and Installing Viber

Before setting up your account, you need to download the app. Viber is available on various platforms, including Android, iOS, Windows, macOS, and Linux. Here's how you can get started:

On Mobile Devices (Android/iOS):

1. **Open Your App Store**

   o   For Android: Go to the Google Play Store.

   o   For iOS: Visit the Apple App Store.

2. **Search for Viber**: Type "Viber" into the search bar and look for the app with the purple speech bubble icon.

3. **Download the App**: Tap the "Install" or "Get" button and wait for the download to complete.

4. **Open the App**: Once installed, tap on the app icon to launch it.

On Desktop (Windows/macOS):

1. **Visit the Viber Website**: Navigate to www.viber.com and click on the "Download" button.

2. **Choose Your Platform**: Select the version compatible with your operating system (Windows or macOS).

3. **Install the Application**: Run the installer and follow the on-screen instructions to complete the installation.

4. **Open the App**: Once installed, launch Viber on your desktop.

Registering Your Viber Account

After downloading the app, the next step is to register your account. Viber uses your phone number as your unique identifier, making it easy for others to find and contact you.

1. **Open the App**: Launch the app on your device.

2. **Enter Your Phone Number**

   ○ Select your country from the drop-down menu.

   ○ Type in your phone number and tap "Continue."

   ○ A confirmation prompt will appear to ensure the number is correct. Confirm to proceed.

3. **Verify Your Number**: Viber will send a six-digit verification code via SMS.

   ○ Enter this code into the app to verify your number.

   ○ If you don't receive the code, you can request a call for verification.

4. **Grant Necessary Permissions**: Viber will ask for permissions to access your contacts, microphone, camera, and notifications. Granting these permissions ensures the app functions properly.

Customizing Your Profile

After registration, it's time to personalize your Viber profile. Customizing your profile makes your account unique and recognizable to your contacts.

1. **Set Your Name**

   ○ Tap on the "Edit" icon or "Profile Settings."

o   Enter your full name or nickname. This name will appear to others on Viber.

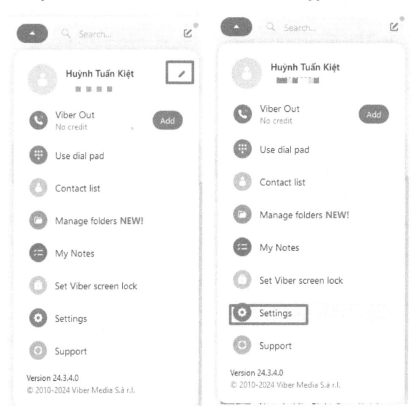

2. **Upload a Profile Picture**

o   Tap on the profile picture placeholder.

o   Choose "Take Photo" to capture a new picture or "Choose from Gallery" to upload an existing one.

o   Adjust the picture to fit within the circle and save it.

3. **Add a Status**

o   Viber allows you to set a short status or mood message.

o   Go to your profile settings and type a status like "Available," "Busy," or something fun.

4. **Link to Other Accounts**: If you want to connect your Viber account with other services like email or social media, you can do so in the account settings.

Syncing Your Contacts

Viber works best when it's connected to your phone's contact list. This allows you to see which of your friends and family members are already on Viber.

1. **Allow Access to Contacts**

    o   When prompted, grant Viber permission to access your contacts.

    o   If you skipped this step during setup, you can enable it later in your device's settings.

2. **Automatic Contact Sync**: Viber automatically scans your contacts and identifies those who already use the app. These contacts will appear in your Viber contact list.

3. **Invite Non-Viber Users**: If some of your friends aren't on Viber, you can send them an invite directly from the app.

    o   Tap "Invite Friends" and choose a method (SMS, email, or social media).

Setting Up Viber on Multiple Devices

One of Viber's standout features is the ability to use the app on multiple devices simultaneously. Here's how you can set it up:

Primary Device (Phone): Your phone acts as the primary device for your Viber account.

Secondary Device (Desktop or Tablet):

1. Download and install Viber on your secondary device.

2. Open the app and choose "Sync with Phone."

3. Scan the QR code displayed on your secondary device using the Viber app on your phone.

4. Once synced, your chats and contacts will be accessible on both devices.

Configuring Initial Settings

To enhance your experience, it's important to configure Viber's settings according to your preferences.

1. **Notifications**

   o   Go to "Settings" > "Notifications."

   o   Customize sound alerts, vibration settings, and notification banners.

2. **Privacy Settings**

   o   Adjust your online status visibility.

   o   Enable or disable read receipts.

   o   Manage blocked contacts.

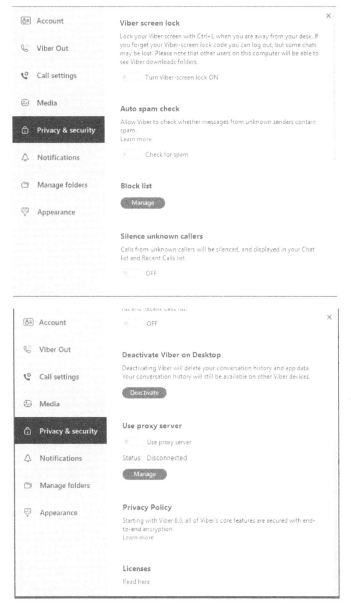

3. **Chat Settings**

   o Choose whether to save media automatically.

   o Customize chat backgrounds and themes.

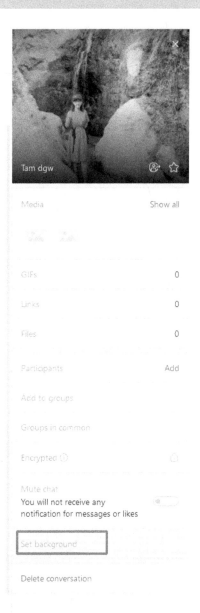

4. Language Settings

o   Go to "Settings" > "Language."

o   Select your preferred language for the app interface.

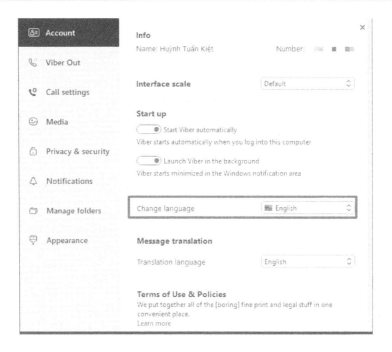

Common Challenges and How to Solve Them

During the setup process, you may encounter some challenges. Here are common issues and their solutions:

1. **Problem: Not Receiving the Verification Code**

   o   Ensure your phone number is entered correctly.

   o   Check your network connection.

   o   Request a call instead of an SMS.

2. **Problem: Contacts Not Syncing**

   o   Ensure you've granted Viber access to your contacts.

   o   Refresh the contact list within the app.

3. **Problem: Unable to Set Profile Picture**

   o   Check app permissions for accessing your camera and gallery.

   o   Restart the app and try again.

Tips for a Successful Setup

- **Use a Reliable Internet Connection:** A stable connection ensures smooth registration and syncing.

- **Double-Check Permissions:** Granting necessary permissions avoids functionality issues later.

- **Explore the App Settings:** Spend time exploring Viber's settings to tailor the app to your preferences.

- **Stay Updated:** Keep your app updated to benefit from the latest features and security enhancements.

Setting up your Viber account is quick and straightforward, yet it's the foundation for all the features you'll explore in the app. Once your account is ready, you'll be all set to dive into the world of messaging, calling, and more!

2.3 Navigating the Viber Interface

Navigating the Viber interface is an essential skill to maximize your experience with the app. Whether you're using it on a smartphone, tablet, or desktop, Viber has a user-friendly design that prioritizes simplicity while offering robust features. In this section, we'll explore the key components of the Viber interface and how to use them effectively.

Understanding the Home Screen

The home screen is the hub of all activity on Viber. It provides access to your chats, calls, and contacts. Here are the main sections you'll find on the home screen:

1. **Chats Tab**: This tab is where you'll see all your conversations. Chats are organized in chronological order, with the most recent conversations appearing at the top. Key features include:

   o **Unread Messages:** Conversations with unread messages are bolded, making them easy to spot.

- o **Pinned Chats:** You can pin important chats to the top of the list for quick access.

- o **Search Bar:** At the top of the screen, the search bar allows you to find contacts or specific messages within chats.

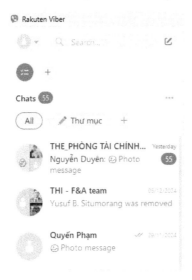

2. **Calls Tab**: The calls tab displays your call history, including voice and video calls. You can also initiate new calls here by tapping the call icon or selecting a contact.

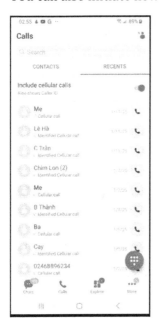

3. **Contacts Tab**: The contacts tab provides a complete list of your saved Viber contacts. Non-Viber contacts are also listed, with an option to invite them to join Viber.

4. **More Tab**: Found on the bottom right (or top right on desktop), this tab offers access to additional settings and features, such as:

  o   Account settings

  o   Privacy options

  o   Themes and customization

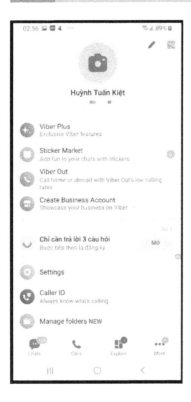

Key Buttons and Icons

Viber's interface relies on intuitive buttons and icons for seamless navigation. Here are some of the most important ones:

1. **Compose Button**: Located prominently on the chats tab, this button allows you to start a new conversation or create a group chat.

2. **Call Icon**: Found on the calls tab, this icon enables you to make a voice or video call.

3. **Search Icon**: Accessible from the top of most screens, the search icon allows you to quickly find contacts, messages, or specific keywords within your chats.

4. **Settings Gear Icon**: Found in the "More" tab, this icon opens the settings menu, where you can manage your account, notifications, and privacy preferences.

5. **Back Button**: This is particularly useful when navigating through different sections of the app, such as returning to the home screen after viewing a chat.

Using the Chat Window

The chat window is where most interactions take place. Here's a breakdown of its components:

1. **Message Input Bar**: At the bottom of the chat window, you'll find the message input bar. This is where you type messages, send stickers, or attach files. Features include:

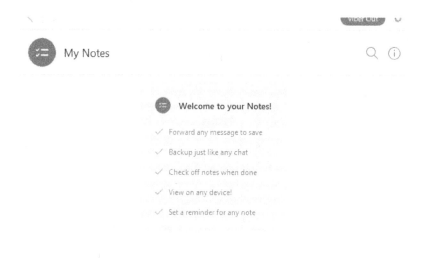

- o **Stickers and Emojis:** Tap the smiley face icon to access Viber's extensive collection of stickers and emojis.

- o **Attachment Options:** Use the paperclip icon to attach photos, videos, documents, or your location.

- o **Voice Messages:** Hold the microphone icon to record and send a voice message.

2. **Conversation History**: The main body of the chat window displays the conversation history. Messages are color-coded, with your messages typically appearing on one side and the recipient's on the other.

3. **Quick Reply Options**: For messages you receive, you'll notice quick reply options like "Like" or "Reply" when you long-press a message.

Exploring the More Tab

The "More" tab serves as a gateway to advanced features and settings. Let's explore its components in detail:

1. **Account and Profile Management**: Here, you can update your profile photo, edit your name, and manage your account settings.

2. **Privacy and Security**: Access options for managing who can contact you, setting up PIN codes for hidden chats, and enabling two-step verification.

3. **Themes and Appearance**: Customize your Viber experience by selecting a theme or changing the chat background.

4. **Additional Features**: The "More" tab also provides links to explore Viber communities, bots, and discover other useful services within the app.

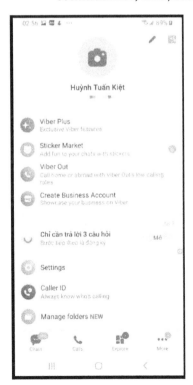

Desktop Interface: A Quick Tour

Viber on desktop mirrors many features of the mobile app while taking advantage of a larger screen. Here's what to expect:

1. **Side Panel Navigation**: The side panel contains shortcuts to chats, calls, and settings.

2. **Multi-Window Support**: You can open multiple chat windows simultaneously, making it easier to multitask.

3. **Quick Access to Attachments**: Drag and drop files directly into the chat window to share them instantly.

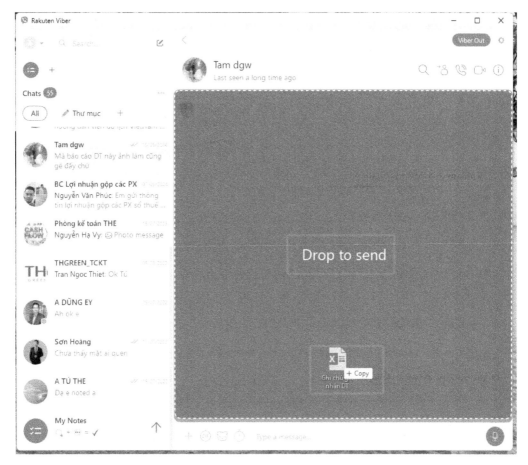

4. **Keyboard Shortcuts**: Desktop users can use shortcuts to perform actions quickly, such as opening a new chat or muting conversations.

Tips for Efficient Navigation

1. **Use Search Features**: The search bar is your best friend for finding contacts or specific messages in large conversations.

2. **Pin Important Chats**: Keep key conversations at the top of your chat list for easy access.

3. **Explore Gestures (Mobile Only)**: Swipe gestures, like swiping left to archive a chat, can save time and streamline your experience.

4. **Customize Notifications**: Tailor notifications for specific chats to stay informed without feeling overwhelmed.

Common Navigation Challenges and Solutions

1. **Lost Chats**

   o **Issue:** Unable to find a conversation.

   o **Solution:** Use the search bar or check the archived chats folder.

2. **Syncing Problems**

   o **Issue:** Messages not appearing on desktop.

   o **Solution:** Ensure you're logged into the same account on both devices and check your internet connection.

3. **Overwhelming Chats**

   o **Issue:** Too many active conversations.

   o **Solution:** Mute less important chats or archive old conversations to declutter your interface.

By mastering the Viber interface, you'll unlock the full potential of the app and enjoy a smoother, more efficient communication experience. Whether you're chatting with friends, making calls, or managing group conversations, understanding how to navigate Viber effectively is the first step toward becoming a power user.

2.4 Syncing Viber Across Devices

Viber is designed to be a seamless communication tool, allowing users to stay connected across multiple devices. Whether you're using a smartphone, tablet, or computer, syncing Viber ensures you never miss an important message or call. This section will guide you through the process of syncing your Viber account across devices, troubleshooting common issues, and maximizing its features for a smooth experience.

Understanding Viber Syncing

Viber syncing allows you to use the app on multiple devices simultaneously. The key advantage is that it keeps your conversations, contacts, and media consistent across all devices. For instance, you can start a chat on your smartphone and continue it on your desktop without interruption. This is particularly useful for people who switch between devices frequently during the day.

To sync Viber effectively, it's important to understand two concepts:

1. **Primary Device**: Your main Viber account is tied to your phone number and is typically installed on your smartphone. This serves as your primary device.

2. **Secondary Devices**: These include any additional devices like desktops, tablets, or other phones where you want to use Viber. These devices sync with your primary device to access messages and calls.

Syncing Viber on Your Desktop

Using Viber on your desktop offers the convenience of typing messages faster and accessing features like file sharing more efficiently. Here's a step-by-step guide to syncing Viber with your desktop:

1. **Download the Viber Desktop App**:

    o Visit the Viber website https://www.viber.com/en/ and download the desktop version for your operating system (Windows, macOS, or Linux).

    o Install the app following the on-screen instructions.

2. **Linking Your Primary Device**:

    o   Open the Viber app on your desktop.

    o   A QR code will appear on the screen.

    o   Open the Viber app on your smartphone, go to **More > Settings > QR Code Scanner**, and scan the QR code displayed on your desktop.

    o   Confirm the sync request, and your desktop app will begin syncing with your smartphone.

3. **Accessing Synced Features**: Once synced, you'll have access to your contacts, chats, and media files on your desktop. You can:

    o   Send and receive messages.

    o   Make voice and video calls.

    o   Share files directly from your computer.

4. **Customizing Desktop Settings**:

    o   Adjust notifications for the desktop app to suit your preferences.

    o   Sync files between your desktop and other devices for quick access.

Syncing Viber on Tablets

If you use a tablet as part of your communication routine, syncing Viber ensures you can enjoy a larger screen and better multitasking capabilities. Follow these steps:

1. **Install the App**:

    o   Download the Viber app from your tablet's app store (Google Play Store for Android or App Store for iOS).

2. **Set Up Your Account**:

    o   Open the app and select **Use as Secondary Device**.

    o   A QR code will appear on the screen.

    o   Scan this QR code using your smartphone Viber app by navigating to **More > Settings > QR Code Scanner**.

3. **Sync Features**:

   o All your chats, calls, and media will appear on the tablet.

   o Use the tablet's larger display for group chats or video calls.

Troubleshooting Syncing Issues

Sometimes, syncing may not work as smoothly as expected. Here are some common issues and how to resolve them:

1. **Error: "Sync Failed"**

   o Ensure your primary device is connected to the internet. Viber relies on your smartphone to sync data.

   o Restart both your primary and secondary devices and try again.

2. **Missing Chats or Media**

   o Verify that your smartphone is running the latest version of Viber. Update the app if necessary.

   o Check storage permissions on the secondary device to ensure it can access media files.

3. **Notification Issues**

   o Notifications may stop syncing properly if the app is closed on the primary device. Ensure Viber is running in the background on your smartphone.

4. **Re-Syncing Devices**

   o If syncing fails repeatedly, unlink the secondary device and re-link it. On your smartphone, go to **More > Settings > Account > Secondary Devices**, select the device, and tap **Unlink**.

Maximizing the Benefits of Syncing

Once your devices are synced, here are some tips to get the most out of this feature:

1. **Use Viber for Work**: With synced devices, you can seamlessly switch between personal and professional conversations. For example, reply to messages on your smartphone during commutes and switch to your desktop during office hours.

2. **Backup and Restore**:

   o   Enable Viber's backup feature to save your chats and media to cloud storage (Google Drive for Android, iCloud for iOS).

   o   This ensures you won't lose important data even if syncing issues occur.

3. **Share Files Easily**:

   o   Send files from your computer to your phone via synced chats. This is especially helpful for sharing documents, images, or presentations.

4. **Enhanced Productivity**:

   o   Use the desktop app for faster typing and multitasking. For example, drag and drop files directly into Viber chats.

Privacy and Security During Syncing

Syncing Viber across devices maintains the app's strong encryption policies, but it's still essential to follow best practices for security:

1. **Enable Two-Step Verification**: Add an extra layer of security to your account by enabling two-step verification under **Settings > Privacy**.

2. **Unlink Unused Devices**: Regularly check the list of secondary devices linked to your account and unlink any you no longer use.

3. **Secure Your Primary Device**: Since your primary device controls access to all secondary devices, ensure it's protected with a PIN or biometric authentication.

Conclusion

Syncing Viber across devices is a game-changer for staying connected seamlessly. Whether you're chatting on your smartphone, making calls on your desktop, or sharing files from your tablet, the ability to sync enhances convenience and productivity. By following the steps outlined above and troubleshooting any issues that arise, you can make the most of this powerful feature. Remember to regularly update your app and prioritize security to ensure a smooth and safe Viber experience.

PART II
Messaging and Calling Essentials

3. Messaging Made Easy

3.1 Sending and Receiving Messages

Messaging is the heart of Viber, allowing users to connect seamlessly with friends, family, and colleagues. With an intuitive interface and a wide range of features, sending and receiving messages on Viber is simple, fast, and enjoyable. In this section, we will explore how to send and receive messages effectively while making the most of Viber's unique features.

Getting Started with Messaging on Viber

Before diving into the details, ensure you've successfully set up your Viber account and synced your contacts. Once this is complete, Viber's messaging feature will allow you to start conversations in just a few taps.

1. **Opening a Chat:**

   o Tap the **"Chats"** tab at the bottom of the screen to view your chat list.

   o To start a new chat, press the **"Compose"** button (usually a pencil icon). Select a contact from your list, or use the search bar to find someone.

   o If the recipient is not on Viber, you'll be prompted to invite them to join.

2. **Typing a Message:**

    o Use the text box at the bottom of the chat screen to compose your message.

    o Viber supports predictive text and autocorrect, which makes typing faster and more accurate.

3. **Sending the Message**:

    o Once your message is ready, tap the **"Send"** button (usually a paper plane icon). Your message will instantly be delivered to the recipient if they are online.

4. **Receiving Messages**:

    o Incoming messages will appear in your chat list with a notification bubble. Tap the chat to open and view the message.

    o You can enable push notifications to stay updated when new messages arrive.

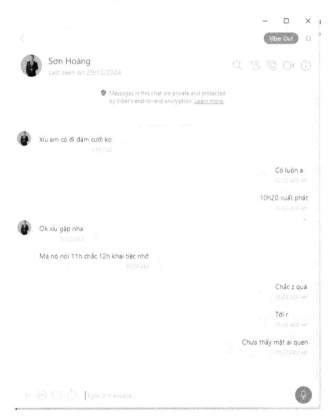

Key Features for Sending Messages

Viber offers several tools to enhance your messaging experience:

1. **Quick Replies**:

   o If you're short on time, swipe left on a message notification to send a predefined quick reply.

2. **Editing Messages**:

   o Sent something by mistake? Long-press on the message and select **"Edit"** to make corrections. Edited messages will be marked with a small "Edited" label for transparency.

3. **Deleting Messages**:

   o If you want to delete a message, long-press it and choose **"Delete for Everyone"** or **"Delete for Me."** This ensures sensitive or incorrect messages can be removed.

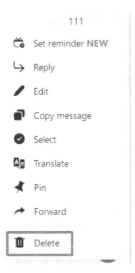

4. **Forwarding Messages**:

   o Share messages with other contacts by long-pressing the message and selecting **"Forward."**

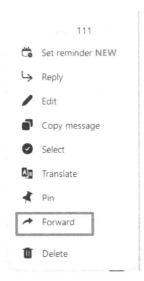

Using Rich Text Features

Viber allows users to customize text messages with formatting options:

1. **Bold Text**: Use asterisks (*) before and after the text (e.g., *This is bold*).

2. **Italic Text**: Use underscores (_) for italics (e.g., *This is italic*).

3. **Strikethrough Text**: Use tildes (~) to strikethrough (e.g., *This is strikethrough*).

These features are particularly useful for emphasizing points in group or professional chats.

Multimedia Messages

Beyond plain text, Viber allows users to send a variety of multimedia content:

1. **Images and Videos**:

    o   Tap the **camera icon** to capture a photo or video instantly.

    o   Alternatively, select the **gallery icon** to send existing media files from your device.

2. **GIFs and Stickers**:

    o   Enhance your messages with fun GIFs and stickers by tapping the **sticker icon**.

    o   Search for specific stickers or use pre-installed sticker packs.

3. **File Sharing**:

    o   Send PDFs, Word documents, and other files by tapping the **attachment icon**.

4. **Location Sharing**:

   o Share your current location with friends for meetups by tapping the **location icon**.

Organizing Your Messages

As your chats grow, organizing them becomes essential:

1. **Pinning Chats**:

   o Pin important conversations to the top of your chat list for quick access. To pin a chat, swipe right on it and tap **"Pin."**

2. **Search in Chats**:

   o   Find specific messages by using the search bar within a chat. Viber supports keyword-based searches, making it easy to locate older messages.

3. **Archiving Chats**:

   o   Archive chats to declutter your chat list. To archive, swipe left on a chat and select **"Archive."** Archived chats can be accessed later from the archive section.

4. **Starred Messages**:

   o   Mark important messages with a star for future reference. Long-press on a message and tap **"Star."**

Message Status Indicators

Viber uses status indicators to show the delivery progress of your messages:

1. **Sent**: A single checkmark indicates your message has been sent.

2. **Delivered**: Two checkmarks mean the message has been delivered to the recipient's device.

3. **Seen**: Two purple checkmarks confirm the recipient has read the message.

Pro Tips for Efficient Messaging

1. **Use Shortcuts**:

- o Viber supports keyboard shortcuts on desktop, allowing you to navigate and send messages faster.

2. **Mute Chats**:

   - o Avoid distractions by muting specific chats. Tap the chat settings and select **"Mute."**

3. **Schedule Messages**:

   - o Send messages at a specific time by scheduling them. Long-press the send button and select the desired time.

4. **Enable Smart Notifications**:

   - o Reduce notification clutter by grouping alerts into a single summary.

Troubleshooting Common Issues

1. **Messages Not Sending**:

   - o Check your internet connection and ensure the recipient's Viber account is active.

2. **Duplicate Messages**:

   - o This issue may occur with unstable connections. Restart Viber or your device to resolve it.

3. **Sync Issues**:

    o   If messages are not appearing across devices, ensure you've enabled sync in the Viber settings.

Conclusion

Sending and receiving messages on Viber is an intuitive and versatile experience, allowing users to connect instantly through text, multimedia, and rich features. By mastering these tools, you can elevate your communication and make the most of everything Viber has to offer.

3.2 Using Stickers and Emojis to Enhance Conversations

In the digital age, communication is no longer limited to words. With the rise of messaging platforms like Viber, emojis and stickers have become integral tools for expressing emotions, conveying humor, and adding a personal touch to conversations. This chapter explores the use of stickers and emojis in Viber, providing practical guidance on how to enhance your messaging experience.

What Are Emojis and Stickers?

Emojis are small digital icons representing emotions, objects, or concepts. They are widely used to add emotion or context to text-based conversations. For example, a simple ☺ can convey happiness, while a 😄 can indicate laughter. Emojis are part of the Unicode standard, meaning they are universally recognized across devices and platforms.

Stickers, on the other hand, are larger, more expressive images, often in the form of cartoons or illustrations. Unlike emojis, stickers are unique to specific platforms and are usually part of themed packs. Viber has a rich collection of stickers that cater to various moods, occasions, and cultural references.

Why Use Stickers and Emojis?

1. **Express Emotions More Clearly**: Text can sometimes be ambiguous. A simple "Okay" can be interpreted in multiple ways—positive, neutral, or even sarcastic. Adding an emoji, such as ☺ or 👍, clarifies the tone of your message.

2. **Add Personality to Conversations**: Emojis and stickers allow you to inject your personality into your chats. A well-chosen sticker can say more than a lengthy paragraph.

3. **Break Language Barriers**: Emojis and stickers are universal. They can convey emotions and ideas without relying on words, making them especially useful in conversations between people who speak different languages.

4. **Make Messages More Engaging**: Adding stickers or emojis can make your messages more visually appealing, keeping your friends or family engaged.

How to Use Emojis in Viber

1. **Accessing Emojis**

   o When typing a message in Viber, tap the **emoji icon** on the keyboard to open the emoji menu.

   o Browse through the different categories (smiley faces, animals, food, activities, etc.) to find the perfect emoji for your message.

2. **Combining Emojis with Text**

   o Emojis can be used as standalone messages or combined with text. For example:

     ▪ "Thank you! ☺"

     ▪ "I'm so excited! 🎉🎉🎉"

3. **Emoji Shortcuts**

   o Some emojis have shortcuts. For instance, typing ":)" will automatically turn into ☺ on many keyboards.

4. **Using Multiple Emojis**

    o   Don't hesitate to string emojis together for extra impact. For example, ▢🎂🎁 conveys a birthday celebration without needing any text.

How to Use Stickers in Viber

1. **Finding Stickers**

   o   Tap the **sticker icon** (usually a smiley face) in the message input area to open the sticker menu.

   o   Swipe through your available sticker packs to find the one you want to use.

2. **Downloading Sticker Packs**

   o   Viber offers free and paid sticker packs. To explore them:

       ▪   Open the sticker menu and tap the **plus icon** or **Store button**.

       ▪   Browse the available packs and download the ones you like.

3. **Sending Stickers**

   o   Simply tap on a sticker to send it. Stickers can be sent as standalone messages or alongside text.

4. **Organizing Sticker Packs**

   o   You can manage your sticker collection by rearranging packs or hiding ones you no longer use. Go to **Settings > Stickers** to customize your collection.

Best Practices for Using Emojis and Stickers

1. **Keep Context in Mind**

   o   While emojis and stickers can enhance conversations, it's important to use them appropriately. For example, a silly sticker might not be suitable in a professional or serious discussion.

2. **Don't Overuse**

     o   Overloading your messages with emojis or stickers can make them difficult to read. Strike a balance to keep your messages engaging but not overwhelming.

3. **Match the Mood**

     o   Choose stickers and emojis that align with the tone of the conversation. For example, a crying emoji 😢 is more fitting for expressing sadness than for celebrating good news.

4. **Explore Seasonal and Event-Based Stickers**

     o   Viber regularly releases stickers for holidays, seasons, and special events. Using these can make your conversations feel timely and festive.

Creative Ways to Use Stickers and Emojis

1. **Tell a Story**

     o   Combine multiple stickers or emojis to create mini-stories or narratives. For example:

        ▪   ☐ → 🍹 → 🏖 → ☐ (Describing a relaxing beach day)

2. **Play Games**

     o   Use emojis to play guessing games or quizzes with friends. For example, send a series of emojis representing a movie or song and ask your friend to guess.

3. **React to Messages**

     o   Use a sticker or emoji to respond quickly to a friend's message without typing anything.

4. **Celebrate Special Moments**

     o   Use celebratory emojis 🎉🎈 or stickers to highlight birthdays, achievements, or holidays.

Customizing Your Sticker and Emoji Experience on Viber

1. **Create Your Own Stickers**

   o   Viber allows you to create custom stickers. Upload your own images or use the Viber Sticker Maker to personalize your chats.

2. **Use Animated Stickers**

   o   Animated stickers bring your messages to life with movement. Check the Viber Sticker Store for available animated packs.

3. **Save Favorite Stickers**

   o   Long-press on a frequently used sticker and add it to your favorites for quick access.

4. **Search for Stickers**

   o   Use the search bar in the sticker menu to find stickers quickly based on keywords or emotions.

Troubleshooting Sticker and Emoji Issues

1. **Can't Find a Sticker Pack?**

   o   Make sure you're using the latest version of Viber. Older versions might not support new sticker packs.

2. **Emoji Not Displaying Correctly?**

   o   This could be due to device compatibility. Check your phone's software and ensure it's up to date.

3. **Sticker Pack Missing?**

   o   If you've accidentally deleted a sticker pack, you can redownload it from the Sticker Store.

Conclusion

Using emojis and stickers on Viber Is an effortless way to make your conversations more vibrant, personal, and engaging. Whether you're sending a simple smiley or a carefully chosen sticker, these tools can help you express yourself in ways that text alone cannot. By understanding how to effectively use and customize them, you can elevate your messaging experience and make every conversation memorable.

3.3 Sending Photos, Videos, and Files

One of the most exciting and convenient features of Viber is its ability to let users share multimedia content seamlessly. Whether it's a photo of a cherished memory, a video capturing a special moment, or an important document, Viber makes sharing these files simple and efficient. In this section, we will explore the step-by-step process of sending photos, videos, and files on Viber, along with tips to optimize your experience.

The Importance of Multimedia Sharing

In today's digital age, communication goes beyond text messages. Sharing photos and videos enhances the emotional connection between users, while sending files supports both personal and professional interactions. Whether you're keeping in touch with loved ones or collaborating with colleagues, Viber ensures that multimedia sharing is quick, secure, and easy to use.

How to Send Photos on Viber

Sharing photos on Viber is incredibly intuitive. Follow these steps:

1. **Open a Chat**

   o Launch the Viber app and select the chat where you want to share your photo. This can be a one-on-one conversation or a group chat.

2. **Access the Photo Feature**

   o Tap the **camera icon** or the **gallery icon** located at the bottom of the chat screen.

   o The camera icon allows you to take a live photo, while the gallery icon enables you to browse through your device's existing photos.

3. **Select a Photo**

o   If you choose the gallery option, browse your images and select the photo you want to share. You can also select multiple photos by holding down on one image and then tapping additional images.

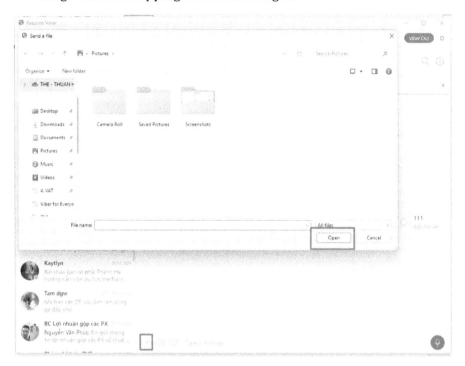

4. **Edit Before Sending** *(Optional)*

    o   Viber includes basic editing tools that let you enhance your photos before sending them. You can:

        ▪   Crop the photo to remove unwanted areas.

        ▪   Add text, drawings, or stickers to make the photo more engaging.

        ▪   Adjust brightness and contrast for better visual appeal.

5. **Send the Photo**

    o   Once you're satisfied, tap the **Send button** (usually a paper plane icon). Your photo will be sent instantly.

Tips for Sending Photos on Viber

- **Compress for Speed:** If you're on a slower internet connection, Viber automatically compresses photos to ensure faster delivery. However, you can adjust settings to send full-resolution photos if needed.

- **Create Albums:** For multiple photos, group them into an album before sending to keep the chat organized.

How to Send Videos on Viber

Sharing videos follows a similar process but with additional considerations for size and length.

1. **Recording a New Video**

   o Tap the **camera icon**, then switch to video mode to record directly within the Viber app. Once you're done, review the recording, trim if necessary, and send it.

2. **Uploading Existing Videos**

   o Tap the **gallery icon** and browse your device for the video you want to share.

3. **Edit the Video** *(Optional)*

   o Viber allows basic video trimming to cut out unnecessary parts.

4. **Send the Video**

   o Tap the **Send button**, and Viber will process and send the video.

Tips for Sending Videos

- **Watch the Size:** Viber supports large files, but if your video exceeds certain size limits, it may need to be compressed.

- **Optimize for Mobile Data:** When using mobile data, choose lower-quality video settings to save bandwidth.

How to Send Files on Viber

Viber isn't just for personal multimedia sharing—it's also an excellent platform for sending documents and files. Here's how to share them effectively:

1. **Locate the File Icon**

   o Open a chat and tap the **attachment icon** (a paperclip symbol). This will display various sharing options.

2. **Browse for Files**

   o   Select the file option and navigate to the location where your file is stored. You can access files from your device storage, cloud services, or even integrated apps like Google Drive or Dropbox (if supported).

3. **Send the File**

   o   Once you've selected your file, tap the **Send button** to share it instantly.

Supported File Types

Viber supports a wide range of file formats, including but not limited to:

- **Documents:** PDFs, Word files, Excel sheets, etc.

- **Images:** JPEG, PNG, GIF, etc.

- **Videos:** MP4, AVI, etc.

- **Compressed Files:** ZIP, RAR, etc.

Best Practices for Sending Files

1. **Check File Size**

   o   While Viber supports large files, some files may require compression for faster sending.

2. **Organize Your Files**

   o   Use descriptive file names to make it easier for recipients to identify the content.

3. **Ensure Security**

   o   Only share files with trusted contacts. Viber encrypts shared files to maintain privacy.

Troubleshooting Common Issues

While sending photos, videos, or files on Viber is generally seamless, occasional issues may arise. Here are some common problems and their solutions:

1. **File Too Large**

   o   If the file exceeds the size limit, try compressing it using a third-party app before sending.

2. **Slow Upload Speed**

   o   Ensure you're connected to a stable Wi-Fi network. Mobile data can be slower and may interrupt uploads.

3. **Unsupported File Type**

   o   If a file isn't supported, convert it to a compatible format before attempting to send it.

4. **App Crashes**

   o   Keep your Viber app updated to avoid bugs that may cause crashes during file sharing.

Benefits of Using Viber for Multimedia Sharing

- **Convenience:** No need for separate apps; Viber integrates all your messaging and sharing needs.

- **Speed:** With compression and optimized uploads, sharing is quick and hassle-free.

- **Security:** End-to-end encryption ensures your shared content remains private.

Conclusion

Sending photos, videos, and files through Viber adds immense value to both personal and professional communication. The platform's user-friendly interface, combined with its robust sharing features, makes it a top choice for multimedia communication. By mastering these tools, you can enhance your messaging experience and stay effortlessly connected with friends, family, and colleagues.

3.4 Using Voice Messages

Voice messages have become an integral part of modern communication, offering a quick and personal way to connect without the need for long calls or typed-out messages. With Viber, voice messaging is both intuitive and feature-rich, ensuring that users can easily communicate their thoughts, emotions, or instructions in their own voice. This chapter explores how to use Viber's voice messaging features effectively, customize them for convenience, and navigate common use cases.

What Are Voice Messages?

Voice messages are short audio recordings that you can send directly within a chat. They are perfect for when typing is inconvenient, such as when you're driving, multitasking, or need to convey emotions that might get lost in text. Viber's voice messaging feature ensures that you can easily record and share your voice with a simple tap.

How to Send a Voice Message on Viber

Sending a voice message on Viber is straightforward. Here's how you can do it:

1. **Open the Chat:** Open the chat with the person or group you want to send the message to.

2. **Locate the Microphone Icon:** On the chat bar, you'll see a small microphone icon next to the text input field.

3. **Press and Hold to Record:**

   o   Press and hold the microphone icon to start recording your message.

   o   Speak clearly into your device's microphone.

   o   Release the button when you're done, and the message will be sent automatically.

4. **Cancel a Recording:** If you change your mind while recording, swipe left (or up, depending on your device) to cancel and discard the recording.

Listening to Voice Messages

When you receive a voice message, it will appear as a waveform in the chat. Here's how to listen to it:

1. Tap the play button on the voice message to listen to it.

2. Use the playback bar to pause, rewind, or fast-forward through the message.

3. Adjust the playback speed if needed. Viber allows you to listen to messages at normal speed or faster.

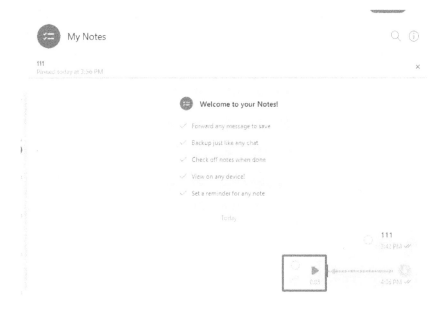

Customizing Voice Message Settings

To make voice messaging even more convenient, Viber offers customization options.

1. **Playback Speed:**

   o In the chat settings, you can adjust the default playback speed for voice messages.

   o Options include 1x (normal speed), 1.5x (slightly faster), and 2x (double speed).

2. **Auto-Download:**

   o You can configure Viber to automatically download voice messages, saving you the hassle of manually retrieving them.

   o Go to **Settings > Media & Storage** and toggle the auto-download feature for voice messages.

3. **Notifications:**

   o Viber notifies you when a voice message is received. You can customize these notifications under **Settings > Notifications** to ensure you never miss an important voice message.

When and Why to Use Voice Messages

Voice messages are ideal for specific situations:

1. **Time-Sensitive Updates:** Share quick updates or instructions without typing.

2. **Emotional Conversations:** Your tone and inflection can convey emotions better than text.

3. **Multitasking:** When your hands are busy, a voice message lets you communicate effortlessly.

4. **Language Barriers:** It's easier to speak a language you're not fluent in rather than typing it out.

For example:

- A parent can send a quick voice message to remind their child to pick up groceries.

- A colleague might use a voice message to explain a complex project detail instead of typing long paragraphs.

Tips for Sending Effective Voice Messages

1. **Be Clear and Concise:** Aim for brevity to ensure your message is easy to understand.

2. **Choose a Quiet Environment:** Background noise can make it difficult for the recipient to hear your message.

3. **Preview Before Sending:** If you're unsure, listen to your recording before sending it.

4. **Use Context:** If the message is part of a larger conversation, provide enough context so the recipient understands the purpose.

5. **Be Mindful of Time Zones:** Avoid sending voice messages late at night unless it's urgent.

Advanced Voice Messaging Features on Viber

Viber offers a few advanced features to enhance the voice messaging experience:

1. **Hands-Free Recording:**

   o Instead of holding the microphone icon, swipe up to lock the recording feature. This allows you to record hands-free.

   o Once you're finished, tap the send button to share the message.

2. **Voice-to-Text Conversion (Optional):**

   o For users who prefer to read rather than listen, Viber provides a voice-to-text transcription feature.

   o After receiving a voice message, tap the "transcribe" option to convert the audio to text.

3. **Multi-Recipient Voice Messages:**

- o Send the same voice message to multiple chats simultaneously using the broadcast feature.

Common Issues and Troubleshooting

While using voice messages, you might encounter a few common issues. Here's how to resolve them:

1. **Poor Audio Quality:**
   - o Ensure your device's microphone is clean and unobstructed.
   - o Use a headset if the built-in microphone is faulty.
   - o Check your internet connection, as poor connectivity can impact audio quality.

2. **Unable to Send Messages:**
   - o Make sure you have granted Viber permission to access your microphone.
   - o Restart the app or your device if the issue persists.

3. **Message Not Playing:**
   - o Verify that your device's sound is not muted.
   - o Try restarting Viber or clearing the app's cache.

Etiquette for Voice Messaging

To ensure smooth communication, follow these etiquette tips:

1. **Ask Before Sending Long Messages:** Some people prefer short messages or typed text, so check with the recipient.

2. **Respect Privacy:** Avoid sending sensitive or confidential information via voice messages.

3. **Be Mindful of Noise:** Try to record in a quiet space to ensure clarity.

4. **Avoid Overusing Voice Messages:** Use them judiciously in professional settings or with contacts who might prefer text.

Real-Life Scenarios of Voice Messaging

1. **Personal Use:**

   o   Sending a heartfelt birthday message to a friend.

   o   Sharing real-time updates while traveling.

2. **Professional Use:**

   o   Explaining a complex idea to a colleague during a busy day.

   o   Responding quickly to a team update during a meeting.

3. **Crisis Communication:**

   o   Using voice messages during emergencies when typing takes too long.

Conclusion

Voice messages are a powerful tool that bridges the gap between text and calls, offering the convenience of asynchronous communication with the personal touch of a voice. By mastering Viber's voice messaging features, you can enhance your communication efficiency, add a personal touch to your messages, and adapt to a variety of scenarios seamlessly. Whether you're chatting with family, collaborating with colleagues, or sending quick updates, voice messages are an indispensable part of your Viber toolkit.

3.5 Organizing Chats and Archiving Conversations

Effective communication goes beyond just sending and receiving messages—it also requires keeping your chats organized and clutter-free. Viber offers multiple tools and features to help users manage their conversations efficiently. In this section, we'll explore how you can keep your chats neat, find old messages when needed, and archive conversations for future reference.

Why Organizing Chats Matters

With time, your Viber chat list can become overwhelming, especially if you use the app for both personal and professional communication. An organized chat list makes it easier to:

- Quickly locate important conversations.

- Avoid missing messages from key contacts.

- Reduce distractions from unimportant or inactive chats.

Whether you're managing personal chats, group conversations, or business-related discussions, these organizational practices can make your messaging experience smoother and more productive.

Pinning Important Chats

Viber allows you to pin essential chats to the top of your conversation list. This feature ensures that your most important contacts or groups are always easy to access.

How to Pin a Chat

1. Open Viber and navigate to your chat list.

2. Long-press the chat you want to pin (on Android) or swipe the chat to the left (on iOS).

3. Select the **"Pin to Top"** option from the menu.

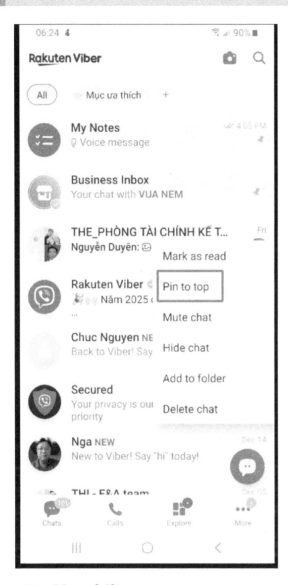

When to Use Pinned Chats

- Pin your family or close friends' group chats for instant access.

- Keep your work-related groups pinned for seamless collaboration.

- Use it for chats with ongoing projects or deadlines.

You can unpin a chat anytime by repeating the process and selecting **"Unpin."**

Categorizing and Grouping Chats

If you're part of multiple group conversations, it's helpful to categorize chats based on their purpose. Although Viber doesn't have folders, you can use naming conventions or customize chat settings to differentiate between personal, work, and hobby groups.

Using Chat Colors and Icons

- Customize group chat icons to make them visually distinct.

- Assign different colors to groups for easy identification.

Renaming Groups

To rename a group chat:

1. Open the group conversation.

2. Tap the group name at the top of the screen.

3. Edit the group name and save the changes.

Pro Tip: Add descriptive keywords to group names, such as "Work Project A" or "Book Club: Monthly Reads," for clarity.

Archiving Inactive Chats

Archiving chats is an excellent way to declutter your main chat list without permanently deleting conversations. This feature is particularly useful for inactive chats that you might need to revisit in the future.

How to Archive a Chat

1. Long-press the chat (on Android) or swipe it to the left (on iOS).

2. Select the **"Archive"** option.

Once archived, the chat will move to a separate "Archived Chats" section, which you can access by scrolling to the bottom of your main chat list and tapping **"View Archived Chats."**

Benefits of Archiving

- Keeps your chat list clean and focused.

- Prevents accidental deletion of important conversations.

- Ensures old messages are easily retrievable.

Searching for Old Messages

Viber's robust search feature helps you quickly locate specific messages or files, even in archived chats.

How to Use the Search Function

1. Tap the search bar at the top of the main chat list.

2. Type keywords, contact names, or phrases related to the message you're looking for.

3. Review the search results, which include chats, messages, and files.

Advanced Search Tips

- Use exact phrases for more accurate results.

- Filter search results by contact name or file type.

- Combine keywords to refine your search further.

Deleting or Clearing Chats

Sometimes, you may want to delete conversations you no longer need to keep your chat list minimal and organized.

Deleting a Chat

1. Long-press the chat (on Android) or swipe it to the left (on iOS).

2. Select **"Delete Chat"** and confirm the action.

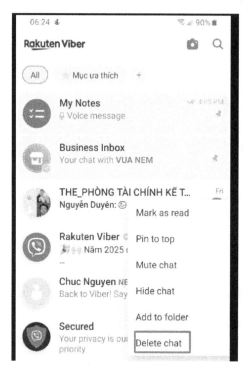

Clearing Chat History

If you want to keep a conversation in your list but remove its contents:

1. Open the chat.

2. Tap the three-dot menu (on Android) or chat settings (on iOS).

3. Select **"Clear Chat History."**

Important Note: Deleting a chat or clearing history is permanent and cannot be undone. Always double-check before taking action.

Muting and Hiding Chats

If you want to reduce distractions without removing chats from your list, consider muting or hiding them.

Muting Notifications

- Open the chat.

- Tap the chat settings menu.

- Select **"Mute"** and choose the duration (e.g., 1 hour, 1 day, or indefinitely).

Muted chats will still appear in your chat list, but you won't receive notifications for new messages.

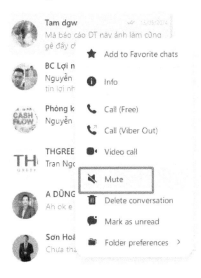

Backup and Restore Chats

To ensure you don't lose your organized chats, it's essential to regularly back up your conversations.

Enabling Chat Backup

1. Open the Viber app and go to Settings.

2. Tap **"Account"** > **"Viber Backup."**

3. Connect your Google Drive (Android) or iCloud (iOS) account.

4. Tap **"Backup Now"** or set up automatic backups.

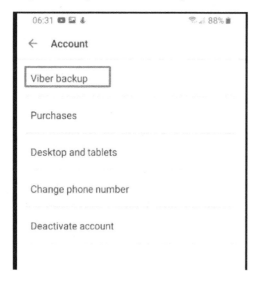

Restoring Chats

If you switch devices or reinstall Viber, you can restore your chats by signing into the same account and selecting **"Restore Backup"** during setup.

Practical Tips for Organizing Chats

1. **Set a Routine:** Spend a few minutes every week archiving or deleting old chats.

2. **Prioritize Active Chats:** Keep frequently used conversations at the top.

3. **Use Search Regularly:** Instead of scrolling endlessly, rely on the search function to find old messages.

4. **Combine Features:** Use pinning, archiving, and hiding together for optimal organization.

Conclusion

Organizing and archiving conversations on Viber helps you stay focused and ensures important messages are always within reach. By utilizing features like pinning, archiving, and searching, you can maintain a clean and efficient chat list. Whether for personal or professional use, these tips will help you master the art of managing your Viber conversations.

4. Calling with Viber

4.1 Making Voice Calls

Voice calls are one of Viber's most popular features, offering users the ability to communicate with crystal-clear audio, no matter where they are in the world. With just a few taps, you can connect with family, friends, or colleagues, whether they're across town or across the globe. This section provides a comprehensive guide to making voice calls on Viber, ensuring you can take full advantage of this powerful feature.

What Are Viber Voice Calls?

Viber voice calls are internet-based, meaning they utilize Wi-Fi or mobile data to connect you with other users. Unlike traditional phone calls, there are no long-distance charges when calling other Viber users, making it an affordable option for staying in touch. If the person you're trying to reach doesn't have Viber, you can use the Viber Out feature to call regular phone numbers at competitive rates.

How to Make a Voice Call on Viber

Making a voice call on Viber is simple and intuitive. Follow these steps to get started:

1. **Open the Viber App**: Launch the Viber app on your device. Ensure you are connected to the internet via Wi-Fi or mobile data.

2. **Select a Contact**

   o   Navigate to the **"Calls"** tab at the bottom of the screen.

   o   Search for the contact you want to call using the search bar or by scrolling through your contact list.

   o   You can also access recent chats and tap the phone icon next to the contact's name.

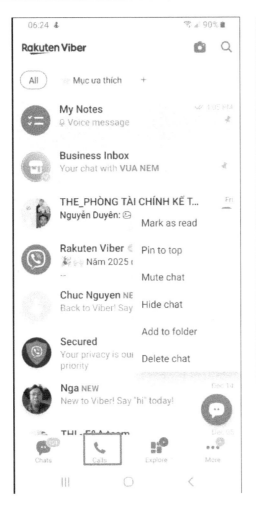

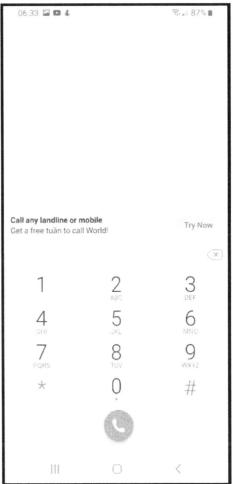

3. **Initiate the Call**

   o Tap the **phone icon** to start a voice call.

   o Viber will ring the selected contact, and the call will begin once they answer.

4. **During the Call**

   o Use the on-screen controls to mute your microphone, switch to speaker mode, or add more participants for a group call.

   o You can also access other apps on your phone without disconnecting the call by pressing the home button.

Understanding the Call Interface

Once the call begins, Viber provides an easy-to-use interface with several helpful features:

- **Mute Button**: Tap to mute or unmute your microphone.

- **Speaker Button**: Switch between the earpiece and loudspeaker.

- **Add Participants**: Turn your call into a group call by adding more people.

- **End Call**: Tap the red phone icon to disconnect.

These options make it easy to manage your calls and adjust settings on the go.

Tips for High-Quality Calls

To ensure the best possible voice call experience, follow these tips:

1. **Stable Internet Connection**

   o A strong Wi-Fi connection is ideal for clear audio.

   o If using mobile data, ensure you are in an area with strong signal strength.

2. **Minimize Background Noise**

   o Use headphones or earbuds to reduce ambient noise and echo.

   o Find a quiet environment for important calls.

3. **Update the App Regularly**

   o Keep your Viber app updated to benefit from the latest performance enhancements and bug fixes.

4. **Check Permissions**

   o Ensure Viber has access to your microphone in the device settings.

Advantages of Viber Voice Calls

Using Viber for voice calls offers several benefits:

- **Cost-Effective**: Free calls to other Viber users make it a budget-friendly choice.

- **Global Reach**: Connect with anyone, anywhere in the world.

- **User-Friendly**: The simple interface makes it accessible for users of all ages.

- **Additional Features**: Group calls, speaker mode, and in-call messaging enhance the experience.

When to Use Voice Calls

Voice calls are perfect for situations where text messages are insufficient or inconvenient. Here are a few scenarios:

- **Quick Updates**: Sharing information that would take too long to type.

- **Personal Connections**: Hearing someone's voice adds a personal touch to communication.

- **Professional Discussions**: Clarifying details during work-related conversations.

Troubleshooting Common Issues

If you experience issues with Viber voice calls, try these troubleshooting steps:

1. **Poor Audio Quality**

   o Check your internet connection.

   o Restart the app or your device.

2. **Call Not Connecting**

   o Ensure the recipient is online and has a stable connection.

   o Verify that you are not blocked by the contact.

3. **Microphone Issues**

   o Confirm that Viber has microphone permissions enabled in your device settings.

   o Test your microphone using another app to rule out hardware problems.

4. **App Crashes**

   o Update to the latest version of Viber.

   o Clear the app cache in your device settings.

Enhancing Your Call Experience

For advanced users, consider these features to make your calls even better:

- **Group Voice Calls**: Add multiple participants to collaborate or chat with friends simultaneously.

- **Custom Ringtones**: Personalize your calls by setting unique ringtones for specific contacts.

- **Viber Desktop**: Use Viber on your computer for seamless transitions between devices.

Alternatives to Voice Calls

While voice calls are convenient, Viber also offers other communication options:

- **Video Calls**: When face-to-face interaction is essential.

- **Text Messaging**: For quick updates or sharing media.

- **Viber Out**: Call non-Viber users when necessary.

Conclusion

Viber voice calls are an essential tool for staying connected, whether you're chatting with loved ones or discussing important matters with colleagues. By understanding the features and best practices outlined in this chapter, you can make the most of your Viber calling experience.

4.2 Using Video Calls

Video calls have become an essential mode of communication in today's digital world, allowing people to see and hear each other no matter the distance. Viber offers a seamless and reliable video calling experience, making it an excellent choice for staying connected with family, friends, and colleagues. This section will guide you through everything you need to know about using video calls on Viber, from setting them up to making the most of their features.

Understanding Viber Video Calls

A Viber video call is a face-to-face conversation through your smartphone, tablet, or computer. Viber uses internet connectivity—Wi-Fi or mobile data—to transmit high-quality video and audio in real time. Whether it's a casual call with a loved one or a professional meeting, Viber's video calling feature offers convenience, clarity, and ease of use.

Setting Up a Video Call

Step 1: Starting a Video Call

1. **Open the Chat**: Navigate to the chat of the person you want to call.

2. **Tap the Call Button**: In the chat window, you'll see a video camera icon. Tap this to initiate a video call.

3. **Wait for the Connection**: Once the recipient answers, your video call will start automatically.

Step 2: Switching from Voice to Video

If you're already in a voice call and wish to switch to a video call:

1. **Tap the Camera Icon**: During the call, you'll see a camera button on the screen.

2. **Enable Video**: Tap the icon to turn on your camera and start transmitting video.

Step 3: Answering a Video Call

When someone calls you via video on Viber:

1. **Incoming Call Screen**: A video preview or caller ID will appear on your screen.

2. **Accept or Decline**: Swipe or tap the "Answer" button to accept the call, or tap "Decline" to reject it.

Optimizing Your Video Call Experience

1. Ensure a Stable Internet Connection

A strong and stable internet connection is crucial for high-quality video calls. If possible, use a Wi-Fi network with good signal strength to avoid interruptions.

2. Check Your Device Setup

- **Camera Placement**: Ensure your device's camera is clean and positioned to show your face clearly.

- **Audio Setup**: Use headphones with a built-in microphone for clearer sound and less background noise.

- **Lighting**: Sit in a well-lit area to ensure the other person can see you clearly. Avoid backlighting as it can obscure your face.

3. Test Your Setup Before Important Calls

If you're joining a critical meeting or a significant call, test your setup beforehand. Check your video and audio settings in Viber's preferences or settings menu.

Exploring Viber Video Call Features

1. HD Video Quality

Viber prioritizes high-definition video to make your calls as lifelike as possible. Ensure your internet connection can support HD video for the best experience.

2. Screen Sharing

During a video call, you can share your screen to collaborate or show presentations. This feature is particularly useful for business meetings or helping someone troubleshoot technical issues.

3. Picture-in-Picture Mode

Viber allows you to minimize your video call window while continuing the conversation. This is helpful when multitasking, such as checking emails or browsing the web during a call.

4. Group Video Calls

You can invite multiple participants to a video call, making it ideal for virtual hangouts, team meetings, or family catch-ups. Simply start a video call and add more people from your contact list.

5. Background Customization

To maintain privacy or add a professional touch to your calls, you can blur your background or use virtual backgrounds. This feature ensures the focus stays on you.

Troubleshooting Video Call Issues

1. Video Not Displaying Properly

- **Check Camera Permissions**: Ensure Viber has permission to access your camera in your device's settings.
- **Restart the App**: Close and reopen Viber to reset the camera functionality.

2. Poor Audio or Video Quality

- **Optimize Your Internet**: Switch to a better Wi-Fi network or move closer to your router.
- **Close Background Apps**: Ensure no other apps are consuming bandwidth or slowing your device.

3. Call Dropping Frequently

- **Update Viber**: Check for updates to ensure you have the latest version of the app.
- **Reconnect to the Network**: Toggle your Wi-Fi or mobile data off and back on.

Using Viber Video Calls for Different Scenarios

1. Personal Use

Video calls are perfect for catching up with family or friends who live far away. The easy interface makes it ideal for users of all ages.

2. Work and Business

For remote teams, Viber video calls offer an excellent way to conduct meetings. Use features like screen sharing and group calls to collaborate efficiently.

3. Education

Teachers and students can use video calls for virtual tutoring sessions or group discussions, ensuring uninterrupted learning.

4. Events and Celebrations

Host virtual events like birthdays or reunions using group video calls. The simplicity of Viber ensures even non-tech-savvy participants can join in.

Tips for a Better Video Calling Experience

1. **Look at the Camera**: Maintain eye contact by looking directly at the camera rather than the screen.

2. **Mute When Not Speaking**: If in a group call, mute yourself to minimize background noise.

3. **Use a Stable Surface**: Place your device on a stable surface to avoid shaky video.

4. **Plan Ahead**: Schedule calls in advance and ensure all participants have the latest version of Viber installed.

Conclusion

Using video calls on Viber is an easy and efficient way to stay connected with loved ones, collaborate with colleagues, or participate in online events. By familiarizing yourself with the steps and features outlined in this section, you'll be well-equipped to make the most of Viber's video calling capabilities. With high-quality video, intuitive controls, and a suite of advanced features, Viber ensures every call is as personal and engaging as an in-person conversation.

4.3 Group Calls: Stay Connected with Multiple People

In today's hyper-connected world, staying in touch with friends, family, and colleagues has never been more important. Viber's **group calling** feature provides a seamless way to connect with multiple people simultaneously, whether for personal catch-ups or professional discussions. This section will guide you through everything you need to know about making, managing, and optimizing group calls on Viber.

1. What Are Group Calls on Viber?

Group calls on Viber allow you to talk to up to **40 participants** simultaneously, making it ideal for virtual gatherings, team meetings, or even study sessions. Unlike traditional calls, group calls provide a shared communication platform where everyone can interact in real time. With Viber's crystal-clear voice quality and robust connection capabilities, group calls are convenient, efficient, and user-friendly.

2. Setting Up a Group Call

Getting started with a group call on Viber is simple and requires just a few taps. Here's how to do it:

Step-by-Step Guide:

1. **Open a Group Chat:** Navigate to an existing group chat or create a new one by selecting the **"New Group"** option. Add the participants you want to include.

2. **Initiate the Call:**

   o Tap the **phone icon** (for voice calls) or the **video icon** (for video calls) at the top of the group chat screen.

   o Viber will notify all members of the group, and those who accept the call will join in.

3. **Add Participants Mid-Call:** If you forgot to include someone, no worries! During the call, tap the **"+" icon** and select additional contacts to invite.

3. Key Features of Viber Group Calls

Viber's group calling functionality comes packed with features designed to make your experience smooth and enjoyable:

- **Mute/Unmute Participants:** As the host, you can mute participants to manage background noise or ensure everyone has a chance to speak. Participants can also mute themselves when not speaking.

- **Switch Between Voice and Video:** Group calls can seamlessly switch from voice to video and vice versa. This is especially useful for presentations or when you need to share something visually.

- **Speaker View and Grid View:** In video calls, toggle between **Speaker View** (focuses on the active speaker) and **Grid View** (shows all participants on screen) for a more customized experience.

- **Screen Sharing (for Desktop):** On Viber desktop, you can share your screen during a group call, making it easier to collaborate on projects or showcase content.

- **End-to-End Encryption:** Like all Viber calls, group calls are **end-to-end encrypted**, ensuring that your conversations remain private and secure.

4. Managing Group Calls Effectively

Hosting a group call requires some management to ensure it runs smoothly. Here are a few tips:

1. Appoint a Moderator: If you're leading the group call, act as a moderator to ensure the discussion stays on track. Encourage participants to take turns speaking and mute participants if necessary.

2. Use Polls for Quick Decisions: For decision-making during group calls, use Viber's **polls feature** in the group chat to gather opinions quickly without interrupting the flow of conversation.

3. Optimize Call Quality: Ensure everyone has a stable internet connection and is in a quiet environment. Encourage participants to use headphones for better sound clarity and reduced background noise.

4. Establish a Structure: For professional group calls, outline an agenda beforehand and share it in the group chat. This helps participants stay focused and ensures the meeting remains productive.

5. Benefits of Using Viber Group Calls

Viber's group call feature has numerous advantages compared to other communication platforms:

- **Ease of Use:** The intuitive interface makes it easy for anyone, even first-time users, to set up and participate in group calls.

- **Cross-Platform Compatibility:** Viber works seamlessly across mobile and desktop devices, ensuring everyone can join regardless of their setup.

- **High-Quality Calls:** With HD voice and video capabilities, you'll experience clear communication, even during calls with large groups.

- **Free to Use:** Unlike many other platforms, Viber group calls are free, even when connecting with people internationally.

6. Common Challenges and How to Overcome Them

While Viber's group calls are highly reliable, you may occasionally encounter challenges. Here's how to address some common issues:

1. Dropped Participants: If someone gets disconnected due to poor internet, encourage them to rejoin by clicking the call link in the group chat.

2. Background Noise: Ask participants to mute their microphones when not speaking. As the host, you can mute participants manually if necessary.

3. Technical Difficulties: Ensure everyone is using the latest version of Viber. Update the app if needed to access the latest features and fixes.

7. Creative Uses for Viber Group Calls

Group calls on Viber are versatile and can be used for a variety of purposes:

- **Family Reunions:** Bring together distant relatives for virtual family gatherings.

- **Virtual Study Groups:** Collaborate with classmates or colleagues to prepare for exams or complete projects.

- **Online Workshops:** Host small-scale workshops or training sessions with interactive discussions.

- **Weekly Check-ins:** Use group calls for regular updates with friends, family, or team members.

8. Frequently Asked Questions About Group Calls

Q: How many people can join a Viber group call? A: Up to 40 participants can join a Viber group call simultaneously.

Q: Can I record a group call? A: Currently, Viber does not have a built-in recording feature. However, you can use third-party software to record calls if needed (with consent from participants).

Q: What happens if I leave the group call? A: If the host leaves, the call continues as long as other participants remain.

Q: Can I join a group call late? A: Yes, you can join an ongoing group call from the group chat by tapping the call notification.

9. Pro Tips for Enhancing Your Group Call Experience

- **Schedule Calls in Advance:** Use the Viber group chat to coordinate and confirm a convenient time for everyone.

- **Use Reactions:** During video calls, use reactions (like thumbs up or heart icons) to interact without interrupting.

- **Test Your Equipment:** Check your microphone, camera, and internet connection before the call begins.

Conclusion

Group calls are an essential part of Viber's functionality, enabling you to connect with multiple people effortlessly. Whether for personal or professional use, mastering group calls on Viber ensures you stay connected, productive, and engaged with the people who matter most. Take advantage of Viber's robust features to make your group calls seamless and enjoyable.

4.4 Call Quality Tips and Tricks

Making high-quality voice and video calls on Viber is one of its standout features. However, ensuring your calls are consistently clear and uninterrupted depends on several factors, from the strength of your internet connection to how well your device is optimized. This section provides detailed tips and tricks to help you get the best possible call quality on Viber.

1. Optimize Your Internet Connection

Use a Stable Wi-Fi Network

A stable Wi-Fi connection is essential for clear calls. If you're experiencing poor call quality:

- **Check Your Wi-Fi Signal:** Ensure you're close to your router for a stronger signal.

- **Avoid Public Wi-Fi:** Public Wi-Fi networks can be slow or congested, leading to interruptions.

Use Mobile Data Wisely

When Wi-Fi isn't available, Viber works seamlessly with mobile data. To optimize your mobile data calls:

- Use 4G, 5G, or LTE networks whenever possible.

- Monitor your data usage, as extended calls can consume significant bandwidth.

- Avoid making calls when the mobile network signal is weak.

Test Internet Speed Before a Call

Low bandwidth can cause lag or dropped calls. Use speed-test apps to check if your network supports a smooth call. A minimum of 1 Mbps for voice calls and 3 Mbps for video calls is recommended.

2. Adjust Viber Call Settings

Enable Low Data Usage Mode

For users with limited internet data, Viber offers a "Low Data Usage" mode for calls. To enable it:

1. Go to **Settings** in the Viber app.

2. Select **Calls and Messages**.

3. Turn on **Low Data Usage for Calls**.

This feature reduces data consumption during calls while maintaining acceptable quality.

Test Video Quality Settings

If you're making a video call and experiencing lags, consider reducing the video resolution:

1. Navigate to **Settings > Media**.

2. Adjust the video quality to "Auto" or "Low" to improve performance on slower networks.

3. Optimize Your Device for Viber Calls

Free Up Device Resources

Lag during calls can be caused by high CPU or RAM usage. To ensure your device is ready:

- Close unnecessary apps running in the background.

- Restart your device regularly to refresh its performance.

Update the Viber App

Ensure you're using the latest version of Viber. Updates often include fixes for bugs and improvements in call quality.

Check Microphone and Speaker Permissions

Viber requires access to your device's microphone and speakers for calls.

- Go to your phone's **Settings** > **App Permissions**.

- Ensure that Viber has microphone and speaker access enabled.

Use Headphones or Earphones

Using wired or Bluetooth headphones can improve audio clarity by reducing background noise and preventing echo.

---

4. Manage Your Environment

Minimize Background Noise

External noise can disrupt call quality. To ensure clear audio:

- Make calls in a quiet environment.

- Use noise-canceling headphones if available.

Ensure Adequate Lighting for Video Calls

For video calls, ensure your environment is well-lit. Natural light works best, but avoid backlighting, which can make you appear shadowy.

---

5. Troubleshooting Common Issues

Dropped Calls

If your calls are frequently dropped:

- Reconnect to your Wi-Fi or switch to mobile data.

- Restart the Viber app to refresh its connection.

Poor Audio or Video Quality

When audio or video quality is low:

- Pause any large downloads or streaming on your network.

- Switch from video to voice-only mode to conserve bandwidth.

Call Connection Delays

If there's a delay in connecting calls:

- Check if the recipient is online.

- Ensure both devices have updated Viber versions.

6. Advanced Tips for Better Viber Calls

Use Viber on Desktop for Long Calls

For extended conversations, consider using Viber on your desktop or laptop. Computers often have better microphones and speakers, leading to improved call quality.

Test Calls Before Important Conversations

Before an important call, make a quick test call to another contact to verify that audio and video are functioning well.

Use a Dedicated Microphone for Professional Calls

For work meetings or professional calls, investing in a USB microphone can significantly enhance audio quality.

7. Stay Updated with Viber Features

Monitor Viber Updates

Viber frequently introduces new features to improve call performance. To stay informed:

- Visit Viber's official blog or website.

- Enable auto-updates for your app on the app store.

Try New Features

Features like "Viber Out" and HD video calls are continuously being improved. Explore these options for better calling experiences.

8. Summary: Key Takeaways for Clear Calls

To ensure optimal Viber call quality:

- Prioritize a strong, stable internet connection.

- Regularly update the Viber app.

- Optimize your device by freeing up resources and enabling permissions.

- Take advantage of headphones and noise-free environments.

- Explore advanced tips for professional-level call clarity.

By following these tips and tricks, you'll be able to make crystal-clear calls on Viber, ensuring seamless communication with friends, family, and colleagues.

4.5 Viber Out: Calling Non-Viber Users

One of Viber's standout features is **Viber Out**, a service that allows you to call people who are not on Viber or do not have an internet connection. With Viber Out, you can make calls to mobile phones and landlines worldwide at competitive rates. This feature is particularly useful when contacting friends, family, or businesses that may not use Viber or even smartphones. In this section, we will explore Viber Out in detail, from setup to maximizing its benefits for your communication needs.

What is Viber Out?

Viber Out is essentially a VoIP (Voice over Internet Protocol) service that extends Viber's functionality beyond internet-based calls. While standard Viber calls require both parties to have the app and an active internet connection, Viber Out lets you reach anyone with a phone number, regardless of whether they use Viber or not.

This service works on a pay-as-you-go basis, requiring you to purchase Viber credit or a subscription plan. The pricing varies depending on the destination, but it is generally much cheaper than traditional international calling rates offered by telecom providers.

How to Set Up Viber Out

Step 1: Accessing Viber Out

1. **Open Viber** on your device (mobile or desktop).

2. Tap on the **More** menu (three horizontal lines or dots).

3. Select **Viber Out** from the list of options.

Step 2: Adding Credit

To use Viber Out, you need to load credit into your account:

1. Go to the **Viber Out** menu.

2. Tap **Buy Credit** or choose a subscription plan.

3. Select the amount of credit you want to add. Options typically range from $4.99 to $24.99, depending on your region.

4. Complete the purchase using your preferred payment method, such as a credit card, PayPal, or Google/Apple Pay.

Step 3: Selecting a Subscription Plan (Optional)

If you frequently call a specific country, Viber offers subscription plans for unlimited or fixed-minute calls to certain destinations. To subscribe:

1. In the **Viber Out** menu, tap **Subscriptions**.

2. Browse available plans by country or region.

3. Choose the plan that best suits your calling needs.

Step 4: Check Your Credit Balance

Before making a call, you can verify your credit balance:

1. Open the **Viber Out** section.

2. Your remaining credit will be displayed at the top of the screen.

Making a Viber Out Call

Step 1: Dialing the Number

1. Go to the **Viber Out** section in the app.

2. Tap the **Dialpad** icon.

3. Enter the number you wish to call, including the country code. Alternatively, you can select a contact from your phonebook.

Step 2: Confirming the Call

1. Viber will display the per-minute rate for the call and the approximate cost based on your current balance.

2. Confirm the call by tapping the **Call** button.

Step 3: Enjoying the Call

During the call, you can use features such as:

- **Mute**: Silence your microphone if needed.

- **Speaker**: Use the speakerphone for hands-free conversations.

- **Keypad**: Enter numbers if you need to navigate an automated menu system.

Step 4: Ending the Call

When your call is finished, simply tap the **End Call** button.

Managing Viber Out Costs

To make the most of Viber Out without overspending, consider the following tips:

1. Monitor Call Rates

- Viber provides transparent pricing for calls to different countries. Always check the rates before making a call.

- Rates are displayed per minute and vary based on the destination.

2. Use Subscriptions for Frequent Calls

- If you regularly call a specific country, a subscription plan can save you money.

- Compare the cost of a subscription to the per-minute rates to determine which option is more economical.

3. Optimize Call Duration

- Keep calls concise to minimize costs, especially for destinations with higher rates.

- Use standard Viber calls whenever possible to avoid charges.

4. Enable Credit Notifications

- Viber can notify you when your credit is running low, so you're never caught off guard.

Understanding Viber Out Features

1. Caller ID

Viber Out supports Caller ID, allowing recipients to see your phone number when you call them. To enable this feature:

1. Go to **Settings** in the Viber app.

2. Select **Caller ID** and follow the prompts to verify your phone number.

2. Call Quality Optimization

Viber Out ensures high-quality calls through its VoIP technology. To maximize call quality:

- Use a stable internet connection (Wi-Fi is recommended).

- Avoid calling from areas with weak cellular data signals.

3. Call History

Viber Out maintains a log of your outgoing calls, including duration and cost. To view your history:

1. Open the **Viber Out** menu.

2. Select **Call History**.

4. Cross-Platform Availability

Viber Out works seamlessly across mobile devices and desktops, allowing you to make calls from anywhere. Simply log in to your Viber account on your preferred device.

Common Issues and Solutions

Problem 1: Credit Not Reflecting After Purchase

- **Solution**: Restart the app and check your balance again. If the issue persists, contact Viber support with your payment receipt.

Problem 2: Poor Call Quality

- **Solution**: Switch to a more stable internet connection. If you're using mobile data, try moving to an area with better coverage.

Problem 3: Unable to Place a Call

- **Solution**: Ensure you have sufficient credit. Also, verify that the number you're dialing is correct and includes the country code.

Problem 4: Call Drops Frequently

- **Solution**: Check for app updates and install the latest version of Viber. Restart your device and retry the call.

Why Use Viber Out?

Viber Out is an excellent tool for staying connected with people worldwide, especially when traditional communication methods are costly or unavailable. Key benefits include:

- **Affordability**: Competitive rates for international calls.

- **Flexibility**: Call anyone, even if they're not on Viber.

- **Convenience**: Manage everything from within the Viber app.

Whether you're reaching out to family abroad, contacting businesses, or staying in touch with friends who don't use Viber, Viber Out provides a reliable and cost-effective solution.

This section ensures you're fully equipped to use Viber Out to its fullest potential, bridging the gap between internet-based and traditional phone communication.

PART III
Advanced Viber Features

5. Group Chats and Communities

5.1 Creating and Managing Group Chats

Group chats are one of the most popular features of Viber, allowing users to communicate and collaborate with multiple people at the same time. Whether you're planning an event, discussing work projects, or simply chatting with friends and family, Viber's group chat feature makes it easy to stay connected. This section will provide a comprehensive guide to creating, managing, and optimizing group chats for all your needs.

Creating a Group Chat

Step 1: Starting a New Group Chat

To create a group chat, follow these steps:

1. **Open Viber**: Launch the Viber app on your smartphone or desktop.

2. **Go to the Chats Tab**: This is the main screen where all your conversations are displayed.

3. **Tap the New Chat Icon**: Look for the pencil icon (on mobile) or the "+" button (on desktop) to start a new chat.

4. **Select "New Group"**: From the options presented, choose "New Group."

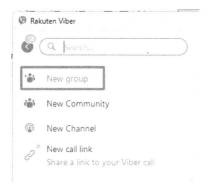

5. **Add Participants**:

   o A list of your contacts will appear. Scroll through or use the search bar to find the people you want to include.

   o Tap on the names of the participants to add them to the group.

   o Viber allows up to **250 participants** in a group chat.

6. **Name Your Group**:

   o Choose a name that reflects the purpose of the group (e.g., "Family Chat," "Project Team," or "Weekend Trip").

   o You can also add a group profile picture by tapping the camera icon next to the group name.

7. **Create the Group**: Once everything is set, tap "Create" to start your group chat.

Managing a Group Chat

Adding or Removing Members

- **Adding Members**:

   o Tap on the group name at the top of the chat screen to access the group settings.

- o Select "Add Participants" and choose new members from your contacts list.

- o Note: Only group admins can add new members unless the group is set to "Public."

- **Removing Members**:

  - o In the group settings, find the list of participants.

  - o Tap on the participant's name and select "Remove from Group."

  - o Be cautious when removing members; consider informing them beforehand to avoid misunderstandings.

Assigning Admins

Admins have special privileges to manage the group, such as adding/removing members, editing group settings, and more.

- To assign an admin:

  - o Go to the group settings.

  - o Tap on a participant's name and select "Make Admin."

- You can have multiple admins in a group for better management.

Changing Group Settings

1. **Group Info**:

   - o Edit the group name, profile picture, or description by tapping the "Edit" button in the group settings.

2. **Permissions**:

   - o Control who can post messages, add members, or change group details.

   - o You can limit these actions to admins only for better moderation.

3. **Notifications**:

   - o Turn on or off notifications for the group.

   - o You can also mute the group for specific durations (e.g., 1 hour, 1 day, or indefinitely).

4. **Pinning a Group**:

  o   Pin important groups to the top of your chat list for easy access.

Using Group Features

Media Sharing

Group chats support various types of media sharing:

- **Photos and Videos**: Tap the camera or gallery icon to share memorable moments.

- **Files**: Send documents, PDFs, or other files directly to the group.

- **Links**: Share links to websites, articles, or other resources.

Using Polls

Polls are a great way to gather opinions or make decisions within a group.

- Tap the "Poll" icon in the chat bar.

- Enter your question and provide multiple answer options.

- Members can vote, and results are displayed in real-time.

Replying and Quoting Messages

In busy group chats, it's easy to lose track of specific conversations. Use the reply feature:

- Long-press a message and select "Reply" to quote it in your response.

- This keeps the conversation organized and clear.

Mentions

To grab someone's attention in a group chat, use the @mention feature:

- Type "@" followed by the participant's name.

- They'll receive a notification about your message, even if they've muted the group.

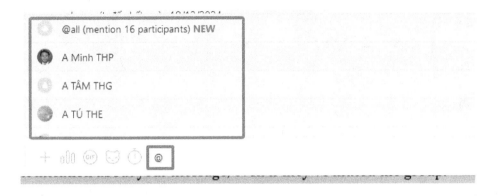

Moderating Group Chats

Rules and Guidelines

- Set clear rules for the group, such as respecting others' opinions and avoiding spam.
- Post the guidelines in the group description or as a pinned message.

Dealing with Spam or Misbehavior

- Remove disruptive members immediately.
- Use Viber's blocking and reporting tools if necessary.

Hidden Chats

For sensitive discussions, consider using Viber's "Hidden Chats" feature:

- Move the group chat to a hidden section accessible only via a PIN.
- This adds an extra layer of privacy for group conversations.

Tips for Successful Group Chats

1. **Keep It Relevant**: Ensure the group remains focused on its purpose.
2. **Use Announcements**: For one-way communication, consider using "Broadcast Lists" instead of group chats.
3. **Engage Members**: Use emojis, stickers, and polls to keep the conversation lively.

4. **Schedule Group Chats**: For planned discussions, agree on a specific time to ensure active participation.

5. **Archive Old Groups**: If a group chat is no longer active, archive it to declutter your chat list.

Common Issues and How to Solve Them

Notifications Not Working

- Check your device's notification settings.

- Ensure Viber has the necessary permissions.

Messages Not Sending

- Confirm you have an active internet connection.

- Restart the app or reinstall it if the issue persists.

Group Chat Limits

- If your group reaches the 250-member limit, consider starting a new group or using Viber Communities for larger audiences.

This section provided a comprehensive guide to creating, managing, and optimizing group chats on Viber. By mastering these features, you can enhance your group communication experience and make the most of what Viber has to offer. In the next section, we'll explore how to maintain privacy and security in your Viber chats.

5.2 Using Polls in Group Chats

Group chats on Viber are more than just a platform to exchange messages; they serve as dynamic spaces where users can collaborate, discuss, and make collective decisions. One of the standout features of Viber group chats is the ability to create and use polls. Polls are a powerful tool for quickly gathering opinions, making decisions, and engaging participants in a fun and interactive way. This section will guide you through the step-by-step process of creating, managing, and effectively utilizing polls in Viber group chats.

What Are Polls in Viber?

Polls in Viber are interactive features that allow users to ask a question and offer multiple options for other group members to choose from. Polls can be used for a variety of purposes, such as:

- Deciding on a meeting time that suits everyone.

- Voting on a topic for discussion.

- Gathering opinions on a particular idea or suggestion.

- Planning group activities like trips or events.

- Adding a fun element to the conversation by asking lighthearted or humorous questions.

How to Create a Poll in a Group Chat

Creating a poll in a Viber group chat is straightforward. Follow these steps to set up your first poll:

Step 1: Open the Group Chat

- Launch Viber on your device and open the group chat where you want to create the poll.

- Make sure the group chat already has members to participate in the poll.

Step 2: Access the Poll Feature

- On the message input bar, locate the **poll icon** (it often resembles a graph or chart).

- If you don't see the icon, tap the "+" sign or menu button to access additional options, where the poll feature will be listed.

Step 3: Enter Your Question and Options

- Tap the poll icon to open the poll creation window.

- Type your question in the **"Question"** field. This should be clear and concise, e.g., "What time works best for our meeting?"

- Add the options for your poll in the **"Options"** field. You can include up to 10 choices depending on the nature of your question. For instance:

    ○ 10 AM

    ○ 2 PM

    ○ 5 PM

- If needed, you can reorder or delete options by tapping and holding on an option.

Step 4: Configure Poll Settings

Before publishing the poll, configure these settings:

1. **Allow Multiple Choices:** Toggle this option on or off, depending on whether you want participants to choose more than one answer.

2. **Anonymous Voting:** Decide if participants' votes should remain private or visible to the group. Enabling anonymity can encourage more honest responses.

Step 5: Publish the Poll

- Once you're satisfied with the question, options, and settings, tap **"Create"** or **"Send"** to publish the poll in the group chat.

How Group Members Interact with Polls

Voting on a Poll

- Group members can vote by tapping their preferred option(s) directly in the poll.

- If multiple choices are allowed, users can select more than one option.

Viewing Results

- The results are updated in real-time as members cast their votes.

- Depending on the privacy settings, participants can either see who voted for each option or just the total number of votes per option.

Changing Votes

- Viber allows participants to change their vote while the poll is active. They can simply tap a different option to update their choice.

Practical Use Cases for Polls

Here are some practical scenarios where polls can be highly effective in group chats:

1. **Planning Events:** Use polls to decide on a date, time, or venue for group events. For example:
   - Question: "Where should we hold the team dinner?"
   - Options: Restaurant A, Restaurant B, Restaurant C.

2. **Making Quick Decisions:** When the group needs to reach a consensus quickly, polls can simplify the process. For instance:
   - Question: "Should we extend the deadline for the project?"
   - Options: Yes, No.

3. **Engaging the Group:** Fun polls can increase engagement and make group chats more interactive. Example:
   - Question: "What's your favorite genre of music?"
   - Options: Pop, Rock, Jazz, Classical, Other.

4. **Collaborative Planning:**

   o   Question: "Which movie should we watch this weekend?"

   o   Options: Movie A, Movie B, Movie C.

Tips for Creating Effective Polls

1. **Be Clear and Specific:** Write a question that is easy to understand and leaves no room for confusion.

2. **Limit the Number of Options:** Too many options can overwhelm participants. Aim for 3–5 choices for straightforward decisions.

3. **Encourage Participation:** Mention the poll in the group chat to make sure everyone knows it's there, e.g., "Hey everyone, please vote in the poll above to finalize our meeting time!"

4. **Use Anonymous Voting for Sensitive Topics:** Anonymity can encourage honest feedback, especially for polls about sensitive issues.

5. **Set Deadlines for Responses:** If the decision is time-sensitive, let participants know when the poll will close.

Managing Polls After Creation

Closing a Poll

- Polls in Viber remain open indefinitely unless closed manually. To close a poll:

   o   Tap on the poll.

   o   Look for the "Close Poll" option (available only to the creator).

Deleting a Poll

- If the poll is no longer relevant, the creator can delete it by tapping and holding the poll message and selecting **"Delete for Everyone."**

Common Questions About Polls

Can I Edit a Poll After Publishing It?

No, polls cannot be edited once they are published. You'll need to create a new poll if changes are necessary.

How Do I Ensure Everyone Votes?

Tag group members or send a reminder message encouraging participation.

What Happens If There's a Tie?

If no clear majority emerges, the group can discuss further to reach a decision or create a follow-up poll with fewer options.

Conclusion

Polls in Viber are a versatile tool that can simplify group decision-making and foster engagement in group chats. Whether you're planning an event, gathering opinions, or just having fun with your friends, polls are easy to create and use. By following the steps and tips outlined above, you'll be able to make the most of this feature and enhance your group chat experience.

5.3 Joining and Participating in Viber Communities

Viber Communities are a unique feature designed to bring people together in a shared digital space, allowing large groups of users to interact, share, and collaborate seamlessly. Whether you're joining a community for hobbies, professional interests, or local events, Viber Communities provide a platform for engaging with others on a global or local scale. This section will guide you through the steps to join, participate, and make the most of Viber Communities.

What Are Viber Communities?

Viber Communities are large group chats where an unlimited number of members can join to share messages, files, and more. Unlike regular group chats, communities allow for enhanced features such as admins and moderators, broadcast messages, and custom rules.

Communities are ideal for fostering conversations around a specific topic or interest, such as fitness, cooking, travel, or professional networking.

Key Features of Viber Communities:

- **Unlimited Members:** Unlike group chats, communities can host an unlimited number of participants.

- **Admin Tools:** Admins have access to moderation tools to manage members, control posts, and enforce rules.

- **Broadcast Messages:** Admins can send announcements to all members simultaneously.

- **Custom Rules:** Communities can set specific rules to maintain order and ensure appropriate behavior.

How to Find and Join Viber Communities

1. **Search for Communities**

   o **Step 1:** Open the Viber app on your device and navigate to the **Explore** tab, represented by a magnifying glass icon.

   o **Step 2:** Use the search bar to type keywords related to the community you want to join (e.g., "Photography," "Fitness Tips," or "Tech News").

   o **Step 3:** Browse through the search results to find communities that match your interests.

2. **Join via Invitation Links**: Many communities are private and require an invitation link to join. You can receive these links through friends, social media posts, or websites.

   o **Step 1:** Tap the invitation link you receive, and Viber will redirect you to the community.

   o **Step 2:** Review the community description and rules.

   o **Step 3:** Click **Join** to become a member.

3. **Discover Through Recommendations**: Viber sometimes recommends communities based on your interests or location. You can find these suggestions in the **Explore** tab or through push notifications.

Understanding Community Rules and Guidelines

Every community has its own set of rules designed to maintain order and respect among members. It's essential to review these guidelines before participating.

- **Examples of Common Rules:**
    - Be respectful and avoid offensive language.
    - Share content relevant to the community's theme.
    - Avoid spamming or posting advertisements without permission.
    - Respect member privacy and avoid sharing personal information.

Breaking the rules can result in warnings, temporary bans, or permanent removal from the community.

Participating in Viber Communities

1. **Introduce Yourself**: Many communities encourage new members to introduce themselves. This is a great way to let others know about your interests and what you hope to gain from the group.

Example:
"Hi everyone, I'm Alex, a travel enthusiast from New York. I'm excited to be here to share tips and learn from your experiences!"

2. **Engage in Conversations**: Actively participating in discussions is key to making the most of your community experience. Here are some tips:
    - Respond to ongoing conversations by replying to specific messages.
    - Start new discussions by asking questions or sharing insights.
    - Use emojis and stickers to make your messages more engaging.

3. **Share Valuable Content**: Communities thrive when members contribute valuable content. Share articles, tips, photos, or videos relevant to the community's theme.

Example:

- In a fitness community, you might share a workout video or healthy recipe.

- In a tech community, you could share the latest gadget reviews or tech news.

4. **Participate in Polls**: Many communities use polls to gather opinions or make decisions. Participating in polls is an easy way to engage with the group and express your preferences.

Example:

- A community might run a poll to decide on the next topic for discussion.

5. **Respect Community Etiquette**

- Avoid dominating conversations or overposting.

- Always credit sources when sharing third-party content.

- Be supportive and encourage others to participate.

Using Advanced Community Features

1. **Tagging Members**: If you want to address someone directly in a community, use the **@username** feature to tag them. This ensures they receive a notification about your message.

Example:
"@JohnDoe, thanks for sharing that article. It was really helpful!"

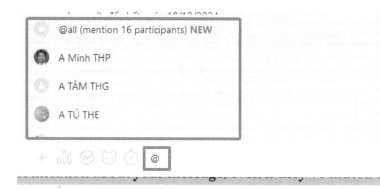

2. **Pinning Messages**: Admins can pin important messages for all members to see. Keep an eye on pinned messages, as they often contain essential information like rules, announcements, or schedules.

3. **Reacting to Messages**: Use reactions (e.g., thumbs up, heart) to show appreciation or agreement with a message. This helps keep the chat lively and interactive.

4. **Reporting Issues**: If you encounter inappropriate behavior or content, use the **Report** feature to notify the admins. This ensures the community remains a safe and respectful space.

Benefits of Participating in Viber Communities

1. **Networking Opportunities**: Communities allow you to connect with like-minded individuals and expand your personal or professional network.

2. **Learning and Growth**: Members often share insights, tips, and resources that can help you learn new skills or stay updated on specific topics.

3. **Building Relationships**: Active participation can lead to meaningful connections, friendships, and collaborations.

4. **Contributing to a Shared Purpose**: Whether it's raising awareness, solving problems, or simply sharing fun content, being part of a community gives you a sense of belonging and purpose.

Leaving a Community

If a community no longer aligns with your interests, you can leave it anytime:

1. Open the community chat.

2. Tap the **Community Info** button (usually an "i" icon).

3. Scroll down and select **Leave and Delete** to exit the community.

Final Tips for Successful Participation

- Be consistent in your engagement but avoid overposting.

- Always respect other members and their opinions.

- Use the platform's tools, like polls and pinned messages, to stay involved.

- Don't hesitate to reach out to admins if you have suggestions or concerns about the community.

By understanding and following these steps, you'll be able to fully immerse yourself in Viber Communities, making them a valuable and enjoyable part of your Viber experience.

5.4 Customizing Group Chat Settings

Group chats on Viber are a powerful way to stay connected with family, friends, colleagues, or even large communities. Customizing group chat settings ensures that your experience is tailored to your preferences, making communication smoother and more enjoyable. In this section, we'll dive into the detailed steps and features available to customize your group chat settings effectively.

---

1. Accessing Group Chat Settings

To begin customizing your group chat settings, follow these steps:

1. **Open the Viber App**

   o Navigate to the group chat you want to customize.

2. **Access the Chat Info Screen**

   o On mobile devices: Tap the group name at the top of the chat window.

   o On desktop: Click the group name or icon in the chat header.

3. **Explore the Settings Options**

   o The settings menu provides various options, including notifications, group info, and administrative controls.

2. Customizing Notifications for Group Chats

Managing notifications for group chats is essential, especially for active groups. Here's how you can personalize notifications:

Mute Notifications

- If you're part of a busy group and don't want constant interruptions, mute the notifications.
- On mobile: Tap **Notifications** > Select **Mute for 1 hour, 8 hours, or Always**.
- On desktop: Right-click the group > Select **Mute Notifications**.

Customize Sound and Vibration

- Change the notification tone for specific groups to differentiate them from others.
- Go to **Settings** > **Notifications** > **Custom Notification Sound** and select your preferred tone.
- On Android, you can also adjust vibration patterns for group notifications.

Smart Notifications

- Enable Smart Notifications to receive a single alert for multiple messages instead of individual notifications for every message.
- This feature is ideal for reducing distractions in highly active group chats.

3. Changing Group Chat Names and Icons

Personalizing the group name and icon can make the chat more recognizable and fun.

Changing the Group Name

1. Go to the group chat info screen.

2. Tap or click the **Group Name**.

3. Enter a new name and confirm by selecting **Save** or pressing **Enter**.

Changing the Group Icon

1. Tap or click the current group icon.

2. Choose to upload a new image from your device or select an emoji or sticker.

3. Adjust the image as needed and save the changes.

This customization helps group members quickly identify the chat, especially when managing multiple group chats.

4. Managing Group Chat Members

Group management tools allow admins to add, remove, or assign roles to members.

Adding New Members

1. Access the group info screen.

2. Select **Add Participants**.

3. Choose contacts from your list or send an invite link.

Removing Members

1. In the group info screen, locate the member list.

2. Tap or click the name of the person you want to remove.

3. Select **Remove from Group**.

Assigning Admin Roles

- Admins can assign co-admin roles to other members to help manage the group.

- To do this:

    1. Tap or click the member's name.

    2. Select **Make Admin**.

- Co-admins can add/remove members, change settings, and moderate the group.

---

5. Managing Media and Files in Group Chats

Group chats often involve sharing photos, videos, and files. Customizing how media is managed helps maintain organization and storage efficiency.

Media Auto-Download Settings

- Prevent automatic downloads of large files to save storage space.

- Go to **Settings** > **Media** > Disable **Auto Download Media in Groups**.

Viewing Shared Media

- To access all shared media in a group:

  o Tap or click **Media Gallery** in the group info screen.

  o This displays photos, videos, and documents in one place.

Deleting Media Files

- Admins can clear media files for all members to free up space.

- In the media gallery, select files and tap **Delete for Everyone**.

---

6. Adjusting Group Privacy Settings

Privacy is critical when managing group chats, especially for larger or public groups.

Approval for New Members

- Enable admin approval for new members to ensure only trusted people join.

- In the group info screen, toggle **Require Admin Approval for New Members**.

Control Who Can Add You to Groups

- Prevent being added to groups without your consent:

  o Go to **Settings** > **Privacy** > **Groups**.

  o Select **Only My Contacts** or customize further.

Hidden Chats

- Move sensitive group chats to the hidden chat section:

    1. Tap and hold the group chat.

    2. Select **Hide Chat** and set a PIN for access.

7. Enhancing Engagement in Group Chats

Using Polls and Surveys

- Create polls to gather opinions or make decisions:

    o Tap the **Poll** icon in the chat.

    o Enter a question and options, then post it to the group.

Pinning Messages

- Pin important messages at the top of the chat for easy access:

    o Tap and hold a message, then select **Pin Message**.

    o Pinned messages are visible to all members.

Customizing Reactions

- React to messages with emojis or stickers to keep conversations engaging.

- Tap and hold a message, then select a reaction from the menu.

8. Backing Up and Restoring Group Chats

Losing important group conversations can be frustrating. Ensure your chats are backed up regularly.

Setting Up Chat Backup

1. Go to **Settings** > **Chats** > **Chat Backup**.

2. Select a cloud storage option (Google Drive or iCloud).

3. Enable **Auto Backup** and set the frequency (daily, weekly, or monthly).

Restoring Chats

- When switching devices, restore your group chats by signing in with the same Viber account and selecting **Restore Chat History** during setup.

9. Tips for Effective Group Chat Management

1. **Set Group Rules:** Use the group description to outline rules for behavior and posting.

2. **Moderate Discussions:** Ensure conversations stay on topic and respectful.

3. **Limit Media Sharing:** Encourage members to use links instead of large files to save storage space.

4. **Regularly Clean Chats:** Delete unnecessary messages and media to keep the chat organized.

5. **Engage Members:** Use polls, pinned messages, and interactive content to maintain interest.

Conclusion

Customizing group chat settings on Viber is key to creating a smooth, enjoyable experience for all members. By taking advantage of the tools and features Viber provides, you can manage group chats effectively, ensure privacy, and foster meaningful interactions. Whether you're organizing a family chat, managing a team project, or moderating a community, these customization options give you the control to make your group chats successful.

6. Privacy and Security on Viber

6.1 Understanding Viber's Encryption and Privacy Features

In today's digital landscape, ensuring the privacy and security of our communications is more critical than ever. Viber takes this responsibility seriously by implementing a range of robust features designed to protect your messages, calls, and personal information. This chapter will provide an in-depth guide to understanding and using Viber's encryption and privacy features, empowering you to communicate safely and confidently.

What Is End-to-End Encryption on Viber?

End-to-end encryption (E2EE) is one of the most essential features that sets Viber apart from many other communication platforms. This technology ensures that messages, calls, and shared content are encrypted directly on your device and only decrypted on the recipient's device.

Here's what this means in practical terms:

- **No Third-Party Access**: Not even Viber itself can read your messages or listen to your calls. This makes your communication private, visible only to you and the intended recipient(s).

- **Automatic Encryption**: Every one-on-one chat on Viber is encrypted by default. You don't need to enable any settings for this feature; it's built into the platform.

How It Works: When you send a message or make a call on Viber:

1. The content is encrypted on your device using a unique cryptographic key.

2. It is transmitted securely to the recipient.

3. Only the recipient's device has the key to decrypt and read the message.

Visual Indicators of Encryption:

- Look for a **padlock icon** next to the contact name in a chat. This indicates that the conversation is encrypted.

What Are Secret Chats on Viber?

If you're looking for an even higher level of privacy, Viber offers a feature called **Secret Chats**. This option allows you to create self-destructing messages, ensuring sensitive content doesn't linger on devices longer than necessary.

Key Features of Secret Chats:

- **Self-Destruct Timers**: Set a timer for messages to disappear after they've been read. Options range from seconds to minutes.

- **Screenshot Protection**: Secret Chats restrict users from taking screenshots, providing an added layer of protection for sensitive conversations.

- **No Forwarding**: Messages in Secret Chats cannot be forwarded, ensuring the content stays within the chat.

How to Start a Secret Chat:

1. Open a chat with the desired contact.

2. Tap on the menu icon (three dots in the top-right corner).

3. Select **Start Secret Chat** from the dropdown.

What Is Hidden Chats on Viber?

Hidden Chats allow you to hide specific conversations from the main chat list, protecting them with a PIN code. This feature is perfect for users who want to add an extra layer of privacy for particular chats.

How to Hide a Chat:

1. Open the chat you want to hide.

2. Tap the menu icon (three dots).

3. Select **Hide Chat**.

4. Set a PIN code if it's your first time using Hidden Chats.

Accessing Hidden Chats:

- To view your Hidden Chats, swipe down on the main chat list and enter your PIN code.

Viber's Additional Privacy Settings

Viber offers a wide range of privacy settings that allow you to control how others interact with you on the platform. Below are the most important settings to configure for maximum privacy:

1. Controlling Who Can Contact You

Viber allows you to manage who can message or call you:

- **Blocking Unwanted Contacts**: If you receive unwanted messages or calls, block the sender by opening the chat, tapping on the three dots, and selecting **Block Contact**.
- **Filtering Messages from Unknown Senders**: In the privacy settings, you can filter messages from people not in your contacts.

2. Disabling "Seen" and "Online" Status

To maintain anonymity or reduce pressure to respond immediately, you can disable these visibility features:

- **"Seen" Status**: Turn off the option that shows others when you've read their messages.
- **"Online" Status**: Hide your online status to appear offline to others.

Steps to Adjust These Settings:

1. Open Viber and go to **Settings**.
2. Select **Privacy**.
3. Toggle off **Share Online Status** and **Send Seen Status**.

3. Controlling Personal Data Visibility

Viber allows you to customize what information is visible to others, including your profile photo, phone number, and "about" description.

- **Setting Who Can See Your Profile Photo**: Options include "Everyone," "My Contacts," or "Nobody."

Two-Step Verification for Added Security

Two-step verification is an additional security layer that prevents unauthorized access to your account. Once enabled, you'll need to enter a unique PIN when registering your phone number on a new device.

How to Enable Two-Step Verification:

1. Open **Settings** in Viber.

2. Tap on **Privacy**.

3. Select **Two-Step Verification**.

4. Set a PIN and add an email address for recovery purposes.

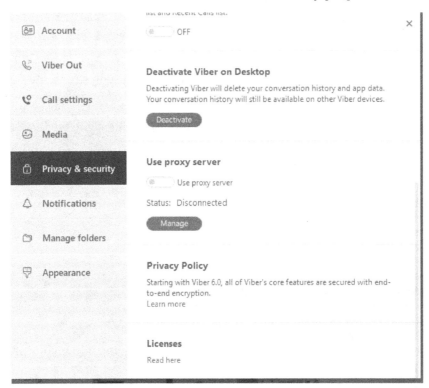

Staying Safe from Scams and Spam on Viber

While Viber's encryption protects your content, you still need to be vigilant against scams or spam messages. Here are some tips:

- **Don't Share Sensitive Information**: Never send passwords, bank details, or other personal data through messaging apps.

- **Report Suspicious Activity**: If you receive a suspicious message or call, report it to Viber by opening the chat, tapping the menu, and selecting **Report**.

- **Be Cautious of Links**: Avoid clicking on unfamiliar links, as they may lead to phishing sites.

Keeping Your App Up-to-Date

To ensure your privacy and security features are up-to-date, regularly update the Viber app. Each update often includes bug fixes and enhanced security protocols.

How to Check for Updates:

- On iOS: Go to the App Store and check for updates.

- On Android: Open the Google Play Store and update Viber.

Conclusion

Understanding Viber's encryption and privacy features ensures that you're using the platform in the safest way possible. By taking advantage of end-to-end encryption, Secret Chats, and customizable privacy settings, you can maintain control over your communications and enjoy a secure messaging experience. In the next section, we'll explore how to block unwanted contacts and manage your Viber interactions effectively.

6.2 Managing Who Can Contact You

Managing who can contact you on Viber is a key part of ensuring a safe and enjoyable messaging experience. With millions of users worldwide, it's important to know how to control your privacy settings to avoid spam, unwanted messages, or potential threats. This chapter will guide you step-by-step on managing your contacts effectively, leveraging Viber's privacy tools to maintain a secure and personalized environment.

Understanding the Basics of Contact Management

Viber provides multiple options for controlling who can contact you. Whether you want to block a specific person, limit how strangers reach you, or customize who can see your profile information, these settings are easily accessible and configurable. Here's a breakdown of what you can manage:

- **Blocking Contacts**: Prevent specific users from messaging or calling you.

- **Filtering Messages**: Control who can send you messages directly.

- **Hidden Numbers for Communities**: Ensure privacy in group chats and communities.

- **Profile Visibility**: Decide who can see your profile picture, status, and other details.

Step-by-Step Guide to Managing Contact Settings

1. Blocking and Unblocking Contacts

Blocking a contact is a straightforward process that prevents the person from calling, messaging, or interacting with you on Viber.

How to Block a Contact:

1. Open the **Viber app** on your smartphone or desktop.

2. Go to the chat of the person you want to block.

3. Tap their name or number at the top of the chat to open their profile.

4. Scroll down and select **Block this Contact**.

5. Confirm your choice when prompted.

Once blocked, the contact will no longer be able to reach you via Viber, and they won't be notified of the block.

How to Unblock a Contact:

1. Open Viber and navigate to **Settings**.

2. Tap **Privacy** > **Blocked Contacts List**.

3. Find the contact you want to unblock and tap **Unblock** next to their name.

Blocking is a great way to stop unwanted communication temporarily or permanently.

2. Adjusting Message Filtering Options

Viber offers message filtering to control who can send you direct messages. By enabling this feature, you can separate messages from your contacts and strangers.

How to Enable Message Filtering:

1. Open the Viber app.

2. Go to **Settings** > **Privacy** > **Message Requests**.

3. Toggle on **Filter Messages**.

When this setting is enabled, messages from people not in your contact list will appear in a separate "Message Requests" folder. You can review these messages and choose to accept or ignore them.

3. Controlling Who Can See Your Profile Information

Your profile picture, name, and status are visible to others on Viber. However, you can control who gets access to this information.

How to Manage Profile Visibility:

1. Open the Viber app and go to **Settings**.

2. Tap **Privacy** > **Profile Visibility**.

3. Choose one of the following options:

- o **Everyone**: Allows all Viber users to see your profile information.

- o **My Contacts Only**: Restricts visibility to people in your contact list.

If you want an extra layer of privacy, always select "My Contacts Only."

4. Managing Community and Group Privacy

Viber communities and group chats allow users to interact with a wider audience. However, this also means that strangers might gain access to your number or profile.

How to Hide Your Number in Communities:

1. Go to **Settings > Privacy**.

2. Scroll to **Communities and Group Chats**.

3. Toggle on **Hide My Number**.

This ensures that only group admins can see your number, offering an added layer of privacy in larger groups.

Controlling Who Can Add You to Groups:

1. Navigate to **Settings > Privacy > Groups**.

2. Choose **Who Can Add Me to Groups**.

3. Select **My Contacts** or **Nobody** to limit unwanted group invites.

5. Reporting and Blocking Spam or Harassment

If you receive spam or harassment, Viber allows you to report and block these users.

How to Report a Contact:

1. Open the chat from the spammer.

2. Tap their name at the top of the screen.

3. Scroll down and select **Report This Contact**.

4. Choose the reason for reporting and confirm.

Reporting helps Viber identify and remove malicious accounts.

Tips for Maximizing Privacy on Viber

1. Keep Your Contact List Updated

Regularly review and update your contact list to ensure it contains only people you trust. Remove outdated or unknown contacts to minimize exposure.

2. Use Two-Step Verification

Enable two-step verification for an extra layer of security. This prevents unauthorized access to your account even if someone gets your phone.

How to Enable Two-Step Verification:

1. Go to **Settings** > **Privacy**.

2. Tap **Two-Step Verification** and set up a PIN.

3. Add an email address for recovery.

3. Be Cautious with Public Communities

When joining public Viber communities, avoid sharing personal information like your phone number or address.

4. Monitor App Permissions

Check what permissions the Viber app has on your device. Limit access to unnecessary data or apps.

How to Review Permissions:

1. Go to your phone's **Settings**.

2. Find **Apps** > **Viber** > **Permissions**.

3. Adjust settings to align with your privacy preferences.

Common Scenarios and Solutions

Scenario 1: Receiving Unwanted Messages

If you frequently receive messages from unknown users, enable **Message Filtering** and block unwanted contacts.

Scenario 2: Being Added to Groups Without Permission

Update your group settings to allow only trusted contacts to add you to groups.

Scenario 3: Suspicious Links or Files

If someone sends you a suspicious link or file, don't open it. Block the sender and report them to Viber.

Conclusion

Managing who can contact you on Viber is essential for maintaining your safety and peace of mind. By taking advantage of the privacy settings, you can create a secure communication environment tailored to your needs. Remember to regularly review and update your settings to stay ahead of potential privacy risks.

6.3 Setting Up PIN Lock and Hidden Chats

Viber is designed with user privacy at its core, offering features like PIN lock and hidden chats to help you safeguard sensitive conversations and maintain control over who sees your messages. This section provides a step-by-step guide to setting up and using these features, along with tips for managing them effectively.

What is a PIN Lock and Hidden Chats on Viber?

- **PIN Lock**: This feature allows you to secure access to specific chats by requiring a four-digit PIN. It's an added layer of security, especially if you share your phone with others or want to keep certain conversations private.

- **Hidden Chats**: Hidden Chats take privacy a step further by removing selected chats from the main chat list. These chats are accessible only by entering a PIN. This is particularly useful for hiding personal or sensitive discussions.

Why Use These Features?

1. **Enhanced Privacy**: Prevent unauthorized access to private conversations.

2. **Organized Chat List**: Keep your main chat screen tidy by hiding less frequently accessed chats.

3. **Customizable Access**: Use a unique PIN to control who can view hidden conversations.

Step-by-Step Guide to Setting Up PIN Lock

Step 1: Enable PIN Lock for Viber

1. **Open Viber**: Launch the Viber app on your smartphone.

2. **Go to Settings**: Tap on the **three-line menu** in the top-left corner (Android) or tap **More** at the bottom-right (iOS). Then, select **Settings**.

3. **Choose Privacy**: In the Settings menu, tap on **Privacy**.

4. **Enable PIN Lock**: Scroll to **Hidden Chats** or **PIN Settings** (depending on the app version) and enable PIN Lock.

Step 2: Set Your PIN

1. **Enter a PIN**: Create a four-digit PIN. Choose a number that is easy for you to remember but difficult for others to guess. Avoid using obvious combinations like "1234" or your birth year.

2. **Confirm Your PIN**: Re-enter the PIN to confirm.

3. **Recovery Options**: Viber may prompt you to set up a recovery email. This is important in case you forget your PIN. Make sure to provide an email address you regularly use.

Step 3: Apply PIN Lock to Specific Chats

1. **Select a Chat**: Navigate to the chat you want to lock.

2. **Open Chat Info**: Tap on the chat title at the top of the screen to open the chat info menu.

3. **Lock the Chat**: Scroll down and select **Hide this Chat** or **Lock this Chat**. Viber will now require the PIN to access this conversation.

Step-by-Step Guide to Using Hidden Chats

Step 1: Hide a Chat

1. **Find the Chat**: Locate the chat you want to hide on your main chat screen.

2. **Long Press or Swipe**: On Android, long press the chat. On iOS, swipe left on the chat and select **Hide Chat**.

3. **Enter Your PIN**: Viber will prompt you to enter your PIN to confirm hiding the chat.

Step 2: Access Hidden Chats

1. **Use the Search Bar**: On the main chat screen, tap the **search bar**.

2. **Enter Your PIN**: Type your PIN in the search bar. This will reveal all hidden chats.

3. **Open the Chat**: Select the hidden chat you want to access.

Step 3: Unhide a Chat

1. **Access the Hidden Chat**: Use the steps above to open the chat.

2. **Unhide the Chat**: Tap on the chat title, scroll down, and select **Unhide Chat**. The chat will now return to your main chat list.

Tips for Managing PIN Lock and Hidden Chats

1. **Use a Secure PIN**: Avoid using common or easily guessed numbers.

2. **Set a Recovery Email**: Ensure you won't lose access to your hidden chats by setting up a recovery option.

3. **Keep Track of Hidden Chats**: Hidden chats are only accessible via your PIN. Make sure to remember which chats you've hidden to avoid confusion.

4. **Regularly Update Your PIN**: For enhanced security, update your PIN periodically.

Additional Features Related to PIN Lock and Hidden Chats

Notification Settings for Hidden Chats

- Viber hides notifications for hidden chats by default. If you want to receive notifications without revealing the content:

    1. Go to **Settings > Notifications**.

    2. Enable **Private Notifications for Hidden Chats**.

    3. This ensures only "New Message" appears on your lock screen.

Customizing PIN Settings

- To change your PIN or recovery email:

    1. Navigate to **Settings > Privacy**.

    2. Select **PIN Settings**.

    3. Update your PIN or recovery email.

Syncing Hidden Chats Across Devices

- Hidden chats and PIN settings sync automatically when you use the same Viber account on multiple devices. Ensure you've set up account sync to keep hidden chats secure across all platforms.

Troubleshooting Common Issues

Forgotten PIN

1. Open the **Hidden Chats** screen and tap **Forgot PIN**.

2. Enter the recovery email you previously set up.

3. Follow the instructions sent to your email to reset the PIN.

Hidden Chats Not Showing Up

- Ensure you're logged into the correct Viber account.

- Verify that you've entered the correct PIN.

PIN Lock Not Working

- Update Viber to the latest version to ensure full compatibility with this feature.

Benefits of Using PIN Lock and Hidden Chats

1. **Protect Sensitive Conversations**: Avoid accidental or unauthorized access to private messages.

2. **Maintain a Clean Interface**: Hide chats you don't use frequently without deleting them.

3. **Peace of Mind**: Know that your conversations are secure even if someone gains temporary access to your phone.

By following the steps and tips outlined above, you'll be able to effectively use PIN Lock and Hidden Chats to enhance your Viber experience while ensuring the utmost privacy and security. These features are simple to use yet powerful tools to keep your communication safe.

6.4 Blocking and Reporting Unwanted Contacts

Viber is a fantastic tool for connecting with people, but as with any communication platform, there may be times when you encounter unwanted contacts or inappropriate behavior. In such cases, knowing how to block and report these contacts is essential for maintaining a safe and secure environment. This section provides a detailed guide on blocking and reporting unwanted contacts on Viber, as well as practical tips to ensure your digital interactions remain positive and secure.

Why Blocking and Reporting Are Important

Blocking and reporting serve two primary purposes:

1. **Protecting Your Privacy**: By blocking a contact, you prevent them from sending you messages, calling you, or viewing your activity status.

2. **Maintaining a Safe Platform**: Reporting contacts who engage in abusive, spammy, or inappropriate behavior helps Viber's team take appropriate action and keeps the platform safe for everyone.

How to Block Unwanted Contacts on Viber

Blocking a contact on Viber is straightforward. Follow these steps depending on your device:

For Mobile Devices

1. Open the chat with the contact you want to block.

2. Tap the contact's name or phone number at the top of the screen to open their profile.

3. Scroll down and select **Block this Contact**.

4. Confirm your action when prompted.

For Desktop (Windows or Mac)

1. Open the conversation with the contact.

2. Click on their name or number in the chat header.

3. Select **Block** from the options.

Once blocked, the contact will no longer be able to send messages or call you, and their messages will not appear in your chat list.

Managing Your Blocked List

Viber allows you to manage your blocked contacts with ease.

To View or Edit Your Blocked List on Mobile:

1. Go to the **More** tab (three horizontal lines or dots).

2. Tap **Settings > Privacy > Blocked Numbers**.

3. You will see a list of all blocked contacts. From here, you can:

- Unblock a contact by tapping their name and selecting **Unblock**.
- Add more contacts to the blocked list by tapping **Add** and choosing a contact.

To Manage Your Blocked List on Desktop:

1. Open the **Settings** menu.

2. Navigate to **Privacy & Security** > **Blocked Contacts**.

3. View, unblock, or add contacts as needed.

Reporting Inappropriate Behavior

If a contact exhibits abusive or spammy behavior, simply blocking them may not be enough. Reporting the behavior ensures that Viber's moderation team can investigate and take necessary actions.

How to Report a Contact:

1. Open the chat with the problematic contact.

2. Tap their name or number at the top to open their profile.

3. Select **Report** and choose the reason for your report (e.g., spam, harassment, inappropriate behavior).

4. Provide additional details if necessary, and confirm the report.

Reported contacts are reviewed by Viber's team. Depending on the severity, they may be warned, restricted, or banned from the platform.

What Happens When You Block or Report Someone?

- **Blocking**:
  - The blocked contact will not be notified.
  - They won't be able to send you messages or call you.
  - They won't see your online status or last seen timestamp.

- **Reporting**:
  - Reports are confidential.
  - Viber will review the reported contact's activity. If their behavior violates Viber's policies, appropriate action will be taken.

Tips to Avoid Unwanted Contacts

1. **Use Privacy Settings**: Adjust your privacy settings to limit who can see your online status or add you to groups. Go to **Settings** > **Privacy** to configure these options.

2. **Be Cautious with Public Communities**: While Viber Communities are a great way to connect with like-minded individuals, they can also attract spam. Avoid sharing personal information publicly.

3. **Restrict Group Invites**: Prevent unknown users from adding you to random groups by disabling group invitations from strangers.

4. **Enable Spam Protection**: Viber has built-in spam detection. Turn it on via **Settings** > **Privacy** > **Spam Protection**.

When to Report Instead of Just Blocking

Not all situations require reporting. Here's when you should consider it:

- **Spam Messages**: Frequent, unsolicited messages promoting products, services, or scams.

- **Harassment or Abuse**: Any form of offensive, threatening, or inappropriate behavior.

- **Impersonation**: If someone is pretending to be you or another person.

- **Suspicious Links**: If a contact sends suspicious links or attachments, report them immediately.

Scenarios and Solutions

- **Scenario 1: Receiving Spam Messages from Unknown Numbers**

- o Solution: Block the number and enable spam protection. Report if the spam is repetitive or harmful.

- **Scenario 2: Being Harassed by a Known Contact**

  - o Solution: Block the contact and report their behavior with a detailed explanation.

- **Scenario 3: Added to Unwanted Groups**

  - o Solution: Exit the group, block the group admin (if unknown), and report the group if it promotes scams or inappropriate content.

Viber's Commitment to User Safety

Viber takes user safety seriously. The platform continuously updates its privacy and security measures to combat spam, harassment, and malicious activities. By blocking and reporting unwanted contacts, you contribute to a safer community for everyone.

Summary

Blocking and reporting are essential tools for maintaining control over your digital interactions on Viber. They empower you to protect your privacy, avoid harassment, and ensure a safer environment. By understanding how to use these features effectively, you can make the most of Viber while staying secure. Remember, your digital safety is in your hands, and Viber provides the tools to help you manage it with ease.

7. Customizing Your Viber Experience

7.1 Changing Themes and Chat Backgrounds

Viber is more than just a communication tool—it's a platform that allows you to personalize your messaging experience to reflect your unique style. One of the best ways to make Viber feel like your own is by changing themes and customizing chat backgrounds. This chapter will guide you through the process of transforming your Viber interface, enhancing not only its aesthetics but also your overall user experience.

Why Customize Themes and Backgrounds?

Themes and chat backgrounds are more than cosmetic features; they play a significant role in improving the usability and appeal of the app. Here are some key benefits:

1. **Personal Expression**: Choose themes and backgrounds that align with your personality or mood.

2. **Enhanced Readability**: A well-chosen theme can make text easier to read, especially for users with visual sensitivities.

3. **Separation of Work and Personal Chats**: Use different backgrounds for work and personal conversations to create a mental boundary between the two.

4. **Better Organization**: Distinctive chat backgrounds can help you quickly identify different conversations.

Exploring Viber Themes

Themes in Viber change the overall look and feel of the app, including the interface colors, fonts, and styles. Here's how to explore and switch themes:

How to Change Themes

1. **Open the Viber App**: Start by launching the Viber app on your device.

2. **Access Settings**: Tap on the three horizontal lines (or "More" tab) in the bottom-right corner to open the menu. Then select **Settings**.

3. **Choose Appearance**: Under Settings, look for the **Appearance** option and tap on it.

4. **Select a Theme**: Viber usually offers a range of built-in themes, including light and dark modes. Choose the one you prefer and tap to apply it.

Dark Mode and Its Benefits

One of the most popular themes is **Dark Mode**, which turns the app's background black or dark gray.

- **Eye Comfort**: Dark mode reduces eye strain, especially in low-light environments.

- **Battery Efficiency**: On devices with OLED screens, dark mode can save battery by using less energy to light up the screen.

- **Modern Aesthetics**: Many users simply enjoy the sleek, modern look of a dark interface.

Customizing Chat Backgrounds

Unlike themes that apply to the entire app, chat backgrounds can be tailored for individual conversations or applied universally to all chats. This feature allows you to add a personal touch to your communication.

Setting a Global Chat Background

1. **Go to Settings**: Access the Settings menu from the app's main interface.

2. **Select Chat Backgrounds**: Tap on the option labeled **Chat Backgrounds**.

3. **Choose a Background**: Viber provides a selection of preloaded backgrounds, ranging from minimalist designs to vibrant patterns. Tap on one to preview and apply it.

Customizing Individual Chats

1. **Open the Chat**: Select the specific chat you want to personalize.

2. **Access Chat Info**: Tap on the three dots in the top-right corner, then select **Chat Info**.

3. **Change Background**: Scroll down to find the **Change Background** option. Choose from Viber's library or upload a custom image.

Using Custom Images as Backgrounds

One of the most exciting features of Viber is the ability to use custom images as chat backgrounds. You can choose a favorite photo, a calming landscape, or even a motivational quote.

Steps to Add a Custom Background

1. **Upload an Image**: Tap the **+** button or **Upload** option in the chat background menu.

2. **Crop and Adjust**: Viber allows you to crop and adjust the image to fit perfectly within the chat window.

3. **Apply and Save**: Once you're satisfied with the preview, tap **Save** to set the image as your background.

Tips for Choosing the Perfect Background

- **Keep It Simple**: Avoid overly busy or cluttered images that might make text hard to read.

- **Match the Mood**: For work-related chats, use professional backgrounds, while personal chats can have more relaxed or playful designs.

- **Optimize for Contrast**: Ensure the text color contrasts well with the background for maximum readability.

Exploring Seasonal and Limited-Time Themes

Viber occasionally offers seasonal or event-based themes and backgrounds, such as holiday-themed designs or special collaborations. These are great for adding a festive touch to your chats or celebrating special occasions.

How to Access Seasonal Themes

1. **Check Updates**: Make sure your Viber app is up to date to access the latest features.

2. **Browse the Theme Store**: Some special themes may appear in the **Sticker Market** or as part of promotional events.

3. **Apply the Theme**: Once downloaded, go to the Appearance settings to apply the new theme.

Troubleshooting Common Issues

While customizing themes and backgrounds is straightforward, you may encounter occasional issues. Here's how to resolve them:

1. **Theme Not Applying**: Ensure you have the latest version of the app and sufficient storage space on your device.

2. **Custom Background Not Displaying Correctly**: Resize or crop the image to match Viber's dimensions.

3. **Reverting to Default**: If you want to reset to the original settings, there's an option in the Appearance menu to revert to the default theme or background.

Maximizing Your Experience

Customizing your Viber themes and backgrounds not only makes the app more enjoyable to use but also improves its functionality. A well-designed interface can boost your productivity, enhance communication, and reflect your personality.

Quick Recap of Tips

- Experiment with themes to find the perfect balance of aesthetics and usability.

- Use distinct backgrounds for different chats to stay organized.

- Leverage dark mode for comfort and efficiency.

- Stay updated with seasonal and event-based themes for a fresh look.

By mastering the art of customizing themes and backgrounds, you'll transform Viber into a platform that truly feels like your own. Whether you're chatting with friends, collaborating with colleagues, or simply enjoying the app, your personalized setup will make every interaction more enjoyable.

7.2 Customizing Notifications

Customizing notifications is one of the most practical ways to ensure that Viber works perfectly for your lifestyle, preferences, and communication needs. Notifications can either enhance your productivity or cause unnecessary distractions if not set up properly. This chapter will guide you through all the ways you can customize Viber notifications to match your personal or professional needs.

Why Customize Notifications?

Viber, like any other communication app, generates notifications for messages, calls, and various updates. While these notifications are helpful in keeping you informed, they can quickly become overwhelming if not managed properly. Customizing notifications allows you to:

- Prioritize important conversations.

- Avoid interruptions during meetings or personal time.

- Reduce noise and distractions from group chats or non-urgent updates.

- Personalize your experience with unique sounds and visual alerts.

By tailoring your notifications, you can strike the perfect balance between staying connected and maintaining focus.

Managing General Notification Settings

To start customizing notifications, you can adjust the general settings for Viber. Follow these steps:

1. **Open Viber Settings:**

   o Launch the Viber app and go to the **More** tab (usually represented by three horizontal lines or dots).

   o Select **Settings** from the menu.

2. **Access Notifications:**

   o Tap on **Notifications** to view all notification-related options.

3. **Adjust Notification Preferences:**

   o **Sound:** Choose your preferred notification tone for messages and calls.

   o **Vibration:** Enable or disable vibration for incoming notifications.

   o **Pop-Up Notifications:** Decide if you want message previews to appear as pop-ups on your screen.

   o **Priority Display:** Choose whether notifications should override other apps or stay in the background.

4. **Preview Messages:**

    o   You can toggle the **Show Message Preview** option on or off. If privacy is a concern, disabling this feature will only display the sender's name in the notification, not the message content.

These general settings allow you to control the basic behavior of Viber notifications across the app.

Customizing Notifications for Specific Chats

If you want a more granular approach to managing notifications, you can customize them for individual chats or groups. This feature is particularly useful if you're part of multiple active groups or have contacts that require immediate attention.

Steps to Customize Chat Notifications

1. **Open the Chat:** Navigate to the specific chat or group you want to customize.

2. **Access Chat Settings:**

    o   Tap on the chat name at the top of the screen to open the chat settings menu.

3. **Modify Notification Preferences:**

    o   **Mute Notifications:** You can mute notifications for a specific period (e.g., 1 hour, 8 hours, or until you turn it back on).

    o   **Custom Sounds:** Assign a unique notification tone for the chat to help you identify messages without checking your phone.

    o   **Priority Alerts:** Enable or disable pop-up notifications or vibration for this chat.

4. **Pin Important Chats:**

    o   You can also pin critical conversations to the top of your chat list to ensure they're easily accessible.

Managing Group Chat Notifications

Group chats can often be a source of frequent and distracting notifications. Viber allows you to control how and when you receive notifications from group chats.

Steps to Customize Group Notifications

1. **Mute Group Chats:**

   o   Open the group chat and access its settings.

   o   Select the option to mute notifications for a specified duration.

2. **Smart Notifications:**

   o   Enable **Smart Notifications** to consolidate multiple messages into a single notification. This feature is ideal for busy groups where multiple members are active simultaneously.

3. **Disable Alerts for Non-Tagged Messages:**

   o   In some groups, you may only want to be notified when someone tags you using "@yourname." This option is available under the group notification settings.

4. **Leave Inactive Groups:**

   o   If a group is no longer relevant, consider leaving it to reduce clutter and notifications.

Choosing Custom Notification Sounds

Viber allows you to personalize your notification sounds to make them stand out. Here's how you can do it:

1. **Access Sound Settings:**

   o   Go to **Settings > Notifications > Sound.**

2. **Select a Tone:**

   o   Choose from the default tones available within Viber or your device's sound library.

3. **Upload Custom Sounds:**

- o If you prefer a unique sound, you can upload your own. This is particularly useful for identifying work-related or personal notifications.

Managing Do Not Disturb Mode

When you need uninterrupted time, Viber's **Do Not Disturb Mode** is an excellent option. Here's how to use it:

1. **Enable Do Not Disturb:**

   - o Go to your phone's settings and enable Do Not Disturb mode. Viber will respect this system-level setting and silence notifications.

2. **Schedule Quiet Hours:**

   - o Viber allows you to schedule quiet hours during which notifications will be muted automatically. This is perfect for nighttime or during meetings.

3. **Override Settings for Important Contacts:**

   - o You can allow specific contacts to bypass Do Not Disturb settings for urgent communications.

Troubleshooting Notification Issues

If you're experiencing issues with notifications, such as delays or missed alerts, try the following:

1. **Check App Permissions:**

   - o Ensure Viber has permission to send notifications in your device settings.

2. **Update Viber:**

   - o Outdated app versions may cause notification glitches. Update Viber to the latest version from your app store.

3. **Clear Cache:**

   - o Clear the app's cache to resolve any temporary issues.

4. **Reinstall the App:**

    ○   As a last resort, reinstall Viber to reset all settings and fix persistent issues.

Best Practices for Notification Management

Here are some practical tips to make the most of Viber notifications:

- Regularly review and update your notification settings as your communication needs evolve.

- Use customized sounds for critical chats or contacts.

- Take advantage of Do Not Disturb mode during meetings, family time, or sleep hours.

- Limit notifications from inactive groups or communities to avoid clutter.

By customizing your Viber notifications, you can create a communication experience that aligns with your lifestyle and ensures you never miss important updates. Whether you're using Viber for personal chats or professional collaboration, these features will help you stay in control and maintain your focus.

7.3 Creating and Using Your Own Stickers

One of the standout features of Viber is its fun and creative sticker library. While the app provides a wide range of stickers for various occasions and moods, the ability to create and use your own stickers adds a personal touch to your conversations. In this section, we'll explore how to design, upload, and utilize custom stickers on Viber, turning your creativity into shareable expressions.

Why Create Your Own Stickers?

Stickers have become an integral part of digital communication, adding emotions, humor, and personality to your messages. Custom stickers allow you to:

1. **Personalize Chats**: Express yourself in a unique way that generic stickers cannot achieve.

2. **Brand Your Communication**: Great for businesses or communities looking to establish a unique identity.

3. **Celebrate Special Moments**: Capture personal moments, inside jokes, or special occasions in sticker form.

4. **Showcase Creativity**: Share your artistic skills and create something fun for your friends or audience.

Step 1: Planning Your Stickers

Before you dive into creating stickers, take some time to plan.

- **Decide on a Theme**: Choose a central idea for your stickers. It could be emotions, your pet, your brand, or anything you love.

- **Sketch Your Ideas**: Draft a few concepts. Simple and expressive designs work best for stickers.

- **Choose Your Tools**: You'll need basic design tools to create your stickers. Some popular choices include Adobe Photoshop, Canva, Procreate, or any drawing software that supports transparent backgrounds.

Step 2: Designing Your Stickers

Creating stickers requires attention to detail. Follow these tips to ensure your designs look professional:

Size and Format

- **Sticker Size**: Viber recommends a size of **512 x 512 pixels** for optimal quality.

- **File Format**: Save your stickers as **PNG files with a transparent background** to ensure they blend seamlessly in chats.

Keep It Simple

- **Bold Lines and Colors**: Use clean lines and vibrant colors to make your stickers stand out, especially on small screens.

- **Focus on Expressions**: Stickers are often used to convey emotions, so exaggerate facial features and gestures for clarity.

Add Text (Optional)

- If your sticker includes text, make sure it's **readable** and **concise**. Use a bold font and avoid clutter.

Create a Set

- Most sticker packs include 5–10 designs. Ensure variety within the theme to make your pack appealing and versatile.

Step 3: Uploading Your Stickers to Viber

Once your stickers are ready, you can upload them to Viber using the Sticker Market feature.

Accessing the Sticker Market

1. Open Viber and navigate to the **Sticker Market** by tapping on the **Stickers icon** in any chat.

2. Select the **Create Stickers** option.

Uploading Your Designs

1. **Choose a Name**: Give your sticker pack a memorable name.

2. **Add Stickers**: Upload your PNG files. Viber allows you to preview how your stickers will look in the app.

3. **Organize Stickers**: Arrange the order of your stickers in the pack for logical flow and ease of use.

Publishing Your Sticker Pack

Once uploaded, you have the option to:

- **Keep it Private**: Use it personally or share it with specific friends.

- **Publish it Publicly**: Make your stickers available for all Viber users to download.

Step 4: Using Your Custom Stickers

After your stickers are uploaded, using them is simple:

1. **Open a Chat**: Start a conversation with a friend or group.

2. **Access Your Stickers**: Tap the **Sticker icon**, and your custom sticker pack will appear in the list.

3. **Share and Enjoy**: Tap on a sticker to send it in the chat.

Tips for Successful Custom Stickers

Creating custom stickers is an art. Here are some tips to enhance your experience:

1. **Test Before Sharing**: Check how your stickers look on various devices. Small details might not appear well on smaller screens.

2. **Gather Feedback**: Share your stickers with friends or a small audience before making them public. Adjust based on their input.

3. **Stay Relevant**: If creating stickers for a business or community, ensure they align with your branding and audience's preferences.

4. **Keep Updating**: Add new stickers to your pack to keep it fresh and engaging.

Common Issues and Troubleshooting

Sticker Not Appearing in Chats

- Ensure the file size is within Viber's limits.

- Check that your stickers are saved in PNG format with a transparent background.

Sticker Quality is Low

- Use high-resolution files. Avoid resizing small images as it reduces quality.

Cannot Upload Stickers

- Make sure your app is updated to the latest version.

- Check your internet connection.

Creative Ideas for Sticker Packs

1. **Celebrate Your Pet**: Turn your pet's cutest moments into a sticker pack.

2. **Embrace Local Culture**: Create stickers featuring popular sayings or cultural icons from your region.

3. **Seasonal Stickers**: Design packs for holidays like Christmas, New Year, or Halloween.

4. **Promote Your Brand**: Include your logo, slogan, and branded imagery to connect with your audience.

Conclusion

Creating your own stickers on Viber is a fun and rewarding way to personalize your conversations and express yourself creatively. Whether you're designing stickers for personal use, to share with friends, or to promote your brand, the process is straightforward and filled with opportunities for creativity. So grab your favorite design tool, unleash your imagination, and let your stickers bring joy to every conversation!

7.4 Personalizing Your Profile

Your Viber profile is more than just a name and photo—it's your digital identity that helps you connect with others. Customizing your profile not only makes it visually appealing but also enhances your experience by reflecting your personality and preferences. In this section, we'll explore how to personalize your Viber profile step by step and ensure it stands out.

Setting Up Your Profile Picture

Your profile picture is often the first thing people notice when they connect with you on Viber. Choosing a clear, high-quality photo can make a great impression. Here's how to set or update your profile picture:

1. **Accessing Profile Settings**

   o Open the Viber app and tap the **More** icon (usually represented by three horizontal lines or dots) at the bottom-right corner.

   o Tap on your name or profile picture at the top of the screen to open your profile settings.

2. **Uploading a Picture**

   o Tap the **Edit** button next to your profile picture.

   o Choose an image from your gallery or take a new photo using your phone's camera.

   o Adjust the image by cropping or resizing it, ensuring your face or the focal point is clear.

3. **Using Creative Profile Pictures**

   o Use vibrant, high-resolution images that reflect your personality.

   o Consider creating a themed profile picture for holidays or special events.

   o If you're a business user, use your brand logo for professional purposes.

4. **Profile Picture Best Practices**

   o Ensure the photo is not blurry or pixelated.

   o Avoid offensive or inappropriate content.

   o Use a consistent image across your communication platforms for easy recognition.

Editing Your Profile Name

Your profile name is how others identify you on Viber. Customizing your name ensures that friends, family, or colleagues can recognize you easily.

1. **Steps to Change Your Name**

   o Go to your **Profile Settings** by tapping your name or profile picture in the More menu.

- o   Tap on the **Name Field** and type your preferred display name.

- o   Save the changes to update your name.

2. **Choosing a Suitable Name**

- o   Use your real name for personal connections.

- o   For a professional context, include your full name or title.

- o   Add emojis or symbols to your name for a fun or creative touch.

3. **Tips for a Memorable Name**

- o   Keep it simple and easy to read.

- o   Avoid using excessive characters or irrelevant text.

- o   Use capital letters appropriately for clarity.

Adding a Short Bio

Your bio is a great way to introduce yourself to your Viber contacts. This feature lets you share a short description, making it easier for people to know more about you.

1. **Where to Find the Bio Section**

- o   In the **Profile Settings**, locate the section labeled **Bio** or **About Me**.

2. **Crafting an Effective Bio**

- o   Keep it concise (1–2 sentences).

- o   Highlight your interests, profession, or a fun fact about yourself.

- o   Use emojis sparingly to add personality.

3. **Examples of Creative Bios**

- o   "Travel enthusiast ✈🗌 | Coffee lover ☕ | Always exploring!"

- o   "Marketing professional by day, gamer by night 🎮"

- o   "Helping businesses grow 🚀 | Contact me for collaborations!"

Setting a Custom Background for Chats

One of the best ways to personalize your Viber experience is by customizing the background of your chats. This feature allows you to add a personal touch to your conversations.

1. **Accessing Chat Background Settings**

    o   Open Viber and go to the **Settings** menu.

    o   Tap on **Chat Backgrounds** to access customization options.

2. **Choosing a Background**

    o   Select from Viber's default background options.

    o   Upload your own photo or image from your gallery.

    o   Use live wallpapers or animated backgrounds for an interactive touch.

3. **Tips for Selecting a Background**

    o   Use subtle patterns or muted colors to avoid distractions during chats.

    o   Match the background with the theme of your profile or interests.

    o   Change backgrounds seasonally or for special occasions.

Personalizing Notification Settings

Customizing how you receive notifications can enhance your Viber experience by aligning it with your preferences and lifestyle.

1. **Setting Up Ringtones**

    o   Go to **Settings > Notifications** and choose a unique ringtone for Viber calls.

    o   Upload your own audio file for a truly personalized ringtone.

2. **Customizing Message Alerts**

    o   Select different notification sounds for individual chats, group chats, and communities.

o   Enable or disable vibration patterns for alerts.

3. **Managing Notification Priorities**

    o   Mute specific chats or groups to focus on important conversations.

    o   Enable smart notifications for summaries instead of every single message.

Adding Fun with Stickers and Emojis

Stickers and emojis are a signature feature of Viber. Personalizing your sticker collection can make your chats more engaging.

1. **Downloading Sticker Packs**

    o   Browse and download sticker packs from the Viber Sticker Market.

    o   Look for seasonal or themed stickers to add variety.

2. **Creating Custom Stickers**

    o   Use the **Create Your Own Stickers** feature in Viber.

    o   Upload personal photos or drawings and turn them into stickers.

3. **Organizing Your Stickers**

    o   Rearrange frequently used stickers for quick access.

    o   Delete or hide sticker packs you no longer use.

Enhancing Your Profile for Professional Use

For users utilizing Viber for work or business, customizing your profile can leave a lasting impression.

1. **Using a Professional Display Picture**

    o   Choose a high-quality photo that reflects your professionalism.

    o   Avoid casual or informal images.

2. **Highlighting Your Role in the Bio**

- Add a brief summary of your job or skills.

- Include links to your business website or portfolio.

3. **Joining Relevant Communities**

- Explore communities related to your industry.

- Actively participate to network and grow your presence.

Conclusion

Customizing your Viber profile is not just about aesthetics—it's about creating a personalized experience that enhances your communication. Whether you're a casual user or a professional, taking the time to personalize your profile can make interactions more enjoyable and meaningful. By following the steps and tips in this section, you'll ensure your Viber profile truly represents you and meets your communication needs.

Would you like to explore advanced features or troubleshoot specific profile issues? Turn to the next chapter for more insights!

8. Exploring Advanced Features

8.1 Using Viber on Desktop

WelcomeHere's a detailed write-up for **Chapter 8: Exploring Advanced Features, 8.1**

In today's interconnected world, staying in touch across multiple devices has become a necessity. Viber, traditionally known as a mobile app, extends its functionality to desktop platforms, providing users with a seamless communication experience. Whether you're working from your laptop, using your home PC, or switching between devices, Viber Desktop ensures that you remain connected, organized, and efficient.

This section explores everything you need to know about using Viber on your desktop, from installation to advanced features that make multitasking a breeze.

Setting Up Viber on Your Desktop

To use Viber on your desktop, you'll first need to install the application and sync it with your mobile account. Here's a step-by-step guide:

1. **Downloading and Installing Viber Desktop**

     o   Visit the official Viber website (https://www.viber.com) to download the desktop version for your operating system (Windows, macOS, or Linux).

     o   Run the downloaded installer and follow the on-screen instructions to complete the installation process.

2. **Syncing with Your Mobile Account**: Viber Desktop works as an extension of your mobile account, so you'll need to link the two:

     o   Open Viber Desktop and click on **"Yes, I have Viber on my mobile"** when prompted.

     o   A QR code will appear on your desktop screen. Open the Viber app on your phone, go to **More > QR Scanner**, and scan the code.

     o   Once verified, your chats, contacts, and settings will sync automatically to your desktop.

3. **System Requirements**: Ensure your computer meets the following minimum requirements for optimal performance:

    o   Windows 7 or later, macOS 10.12 or later, or a compatible Linux distribution.

    o   At least 4GB of RAM and a stable internet connection.

Navigating the Desktop Interface

The Viber desktop interface is designed for simplicity and functionality. Here are its main components:

1. **Sidebar Navigation**

    o   The left-hand sidebar contains quick access to **Chats**, **Contacts**, **Calls**, and **Settings**.

    o   You can also find shortcuts to Viber Communities and Groups for instant communication.

2. **Chat Panel**

    o   The main window displays your active conversations. Click on a chat to open the conversation in full view.

    o   The interface supports drag-and-drop functionality for sharing files directly from your desktop.

3. **Top Menu**

    o   Access additional options such as managing notifications, searching conversations, and adjusting account settings.

Messaging on Desktop

The desktop version of Viber offers all the essential messaging features available on mobile, with added convenience for those working on larger screens.

1. **Sending Text Messages**

- o Compose and send messages quickly using your keyboard. You can also use emojis and stickers directly from the desktop interface.

- o Highlight text and use keyboard shortcuts (e.g., Ctrl + B for bold) to format messages.

2. **Sharing Files and Media**

- o Easily share photos, videos, documents, and other files by dragging and dropping them into the chat window.

- o Files are automatically synced across devices, ensuring recipients can view them on any platform.

3. **Search and Filters**

- o Use the search bar to locate messages, media, or contacts across all your chats. Filters help narrow down results for faster navigation.

Making Calls on Desktop

Viber Desktop is a powerful tool for both personal and professional calls, offering high-quality voice and video calling.

1. **Voice Calls**

- o Click on the **Call** button in any chat to start a voice call. The desktop version provides excellent call clarity with fewer interruptions.

- o Use a headset or external microphone for the best audio experience.

2. **Video Calls**

- o Start a video call by clicking on the camera icon in a chat. You can adjust your camera settings and resolution from the desktop app's settings menu.

- o The larger screen of a desktop enhances the video call experience, especially for group meetings.

3. **Group Calls**

- o Initiate group calls directly from group chats. The desktop interface displays all participants in a grid layout, making it easier to interact.

4. **Viber Out on Desktop**

   o Use Viber Out to call non-Viber users or landline numbers at affordable rates. Top up your Viber Out credit through the desktop app for convenience.

Syncing Across Devices

One of Viber's greatest strengths is its ability to sync seamlessly across devices.

1. **Real-Time Syncing**

   o Messages, calls, and settings are updated in real-time between your desktop and mobile devices.

   o Start a conversation on your phone and continue it on your computer without missing a beat.

2. **Accessing Media Files**

   o View all shared media files in a conversation by opening the **Media Gallery** in the desktop app. This feature ensures you can download or forward files with ease.

3. **Notification Management**

   o Manage notifications independently on your desktop and mobile devices. For example, mute notifications on your phone while working on your computer.

Advanced Desktop Features

The desktop version of Viber includes advanced features to enhance productivity and convenience.

1. **Shortcuts and Quick Replies**

   o Use customizable keyboard shortcuts for faster navigation. For instance, assign shortcuts to open specific chats or perform actions like muting a conversation.

o Enable quick replies to respond to messages directly from desktop notifications.

2. **Screen Sharing**

   o During video calls, you can share your screen with other participants. This feature is particularly useful for remote work or presentations.

3. **Custom Themes**

   o Personalize your desktop app by selecting custom themes and chat backgrounds. Themes sync across devices for a unified appearance.

4. **Integrations and Bots**

   o Explore Viber bots and third-party integrations through the desktop app. These can help automate tasks, provide updates, or even entertain you during breaks.

Tips for Using Viber on Desktop Efficiently

- **Optimize Notifications**: Adjust desktop notifications to minimize distractions while staying informed.

- **Keyboard Shortcuts**: Learn and use keyboard shortcuts to navigate the app quickly.

- **Regular Updates**: Keep your desktop app updated to access new features and security improvements.

- **Data Backup**: Periodically back up your chats on your mobile app to ensure data safety.

Conclusion

Viber Desktop is more than just a mirror of its mobile counterpart; it's a powerful tool that enhances your communication experience. Whether you're using it for casual chats or professional meetings, the desktop version ensures that you stay connected across all your devices. By exploring its advanced features and customizing your setup, you can make the most of what Viber Desktop has to offer.

8.2 Scheduling Messages

Scheduling messages is one of Viber's advanced features that allows users to plan and send messages at a specific time and date. This feature is highly beneficial for both personal and professional communication, ensuring that important messages are sent on time without the need to manually remember and execute the task. Whether it's sending birthday wishes at midnight, reminding a colleague about a meeting, or confirming a delivery time, scheduling messages can make your life more organized and efficient.

What is Message Scheduling?

Message scheduling in Viber allows you to draft a message and set a specific time for it to be automatically sent. Once scheduled, the message remains in a queue until the set time, ensuring that it is delivered exactly when you want it to be. This feature eliminates the risk of forgetting to send timely reminders or greetings, making it a valuable tool for users who want to enhance their communication efficiency.

How to Schedule Messages in Viber

Using the message scheduling feature in Viber is simple and straightforward. Below are the step-by-step instructions:

1. Open a Chat

- Open Viber and navigate to the conversation where you want to send the scheduled message.

- This can be an individual chat or a group chat.

2. Draft Your Message

- Type the message you want to schedule in the message box, just as you would for any normal message.

- Make sure the message is clear, concise, and appropriately tailored for the recipient.

3. Access the Scheduling Option

- Tap and hold the "Send" button (usually shaped like an arrow).

- A menu or pop-up will appear with options, including "Schedule Message."

4. Set the Date and Time

- Select the "Schedule Message" option.

- A calendar and clock interface will appear, allowing you to pick the exact date and time for the message to be sent.

- Confirm your selection.

5. Confirm and Save

- Once the date and time are set, tap "Save" or "Confirm" to finalize the scheduling process.

- The message will now appear in the chat as a scheduled message, often with a clock icon to indicate that it is queued for future delivery.

Editing or Canceling Scheduled Messages

Viber offers flexibility in managing your scheduled messages. Here's how you can edit or cancel them:

1. Access the Scheduled Message

- Navigate to the chat where the message was scheduled.

- Locate the scheduled message, which will typically appear at the bottom of the chat with a timestamp indicating when it will be sent.

2. Edit the Message

- Tap and hold the scheduled message.

- Select the "Edit" option from the menu.

- Modify the text, date, or time as needed and save your changes.

3. Cancel the Message

- If you no longer wish to send the message, tap and hold it and select "Cancel."

- Confirm your decision, and the message will be removed from the queue.

Practical Use Cases for Scheduling Messages

1. Personal Communication

- **Birthday Wishes and Anniversaries:** Never forget to send timely wishes to loved ones. Schedule birthday messages in advance to make sure your greetings arrive at the perfect moment.

- **Reminders for Family and Friends:** Remind someone to pick up groceries, attend an event, or prepare for an important occasion.

2. Professional Communication

- **Meeting Reminders:** Schedule reminders for team members or colleagues about upcoming meetings, deadlines, or important tasks.

- **Project Updates:** Keep your team informed about project milestones by scheduling regular updates.

- **Client Communication:** Send timely updates, confirmations, or follow-ups to clients, ensuring professionalism and reliability.

3. Event Planning

- **Invitations:** Schedule invitations to events like parties, meetings, or webinars to ensure that they're sent at the right time.

- **Follow-Up Messages:** After an event, schedule thank-you messages or feedback requests to attendees.

Tips for Effectively Using Message Scheduling

1. Plan in Advance

Take advantage of scheduling by planning your messages ahead of time. This is especially helpful for time-sensitive communications or when managing multiple tasks.

2. Double-Check Your Message

Always review your message for accuracy before scheduling it. Check for typos, proper dates, and relevance to the recipient.

3. Be Mindful of Time Zones

When communicating with people in different time zones, ensure that the scheduled message aligns with their local time for maximum impact.

4. Avoid Over-Scheduling

While scheduling can be convenient, avoid overusing it. Ensure that your messages still feel personal and thoughtful.

Limitations of Message Scheduling

While the scheduling feature is incredibly useful, there are a few limitations to be aware of:

1. Limited Customization

Viber's scheduling feature may not support recurring messages or advanced automation. For example, you cannot set a daily or weekly schedule for a message.

2. No Notifications for Scheduled Messages

You won't receive a notification when a scheduled message is sent. Make sure to keep track of your scheduled messages to avoid confusion.

3. Device Dependency

The scheduling feature relies on the app being functional and connected to the internet. Ensure that your device remains active for the scheduled message to be delivered.

How Scheduling Messages Enhances Productivity

1. Saves Time

Scheduling messages reduces the need to manually send reminders or updates, freeing up your time for other tasks.

2. Improves Communication Consistency

By scheduling important messages, you ensure that your communication remains timely and reliable.

3. Enhances Professionalism

For businesses, scheduling ensures that clients, colleagues, or customers receive well-timed and thoughtful messages, leaving a positive impression.

4. Reduces Mental Load

Knowing that your messages are pre-planned and scheduled helps reduce the stress of remembering every small detail, allowing you to focus on other priorities.

Conclusion

Scheduling messages in Viber is a powerful yet simple tool that can transform the way you communicate. By mastering this feature, you can ensure that your messages are always timely, professional, and thoughtful. Whether you're using Viber for personal or professional communication, scheduling messages can help you stay organized, productive, and stress-free.

Now that you've learned how to schedule messages, let's explore even more advanced features in the next section!

8.3 Managing Multiple Accounts

Managing multiple accounts on Viber is a convenient feature for users who wish to separate their personal and professional lives or have multiple identities for various purposes. Whether you're a business professional, a freelancer, or just someone who needs a separate account for specific contacts, Viber provides flexible options for handling multiple accounts effectively. This section will guide you through the benefits, setup process, and tips for managing multiple Viber accounts with ease.

Why Use Multiple Viber Accounts?

Before diving into the technicalities, it's essential to understand why managing multiple Viber accounts might be beneficial:

1. **Personal and Professional Separation**: Many people prefer to keep their personal and work lives separate. Having two Viber accounts ensures that your work-related messages and calls don't mix with your personal communications.

2. **Managing Multiple Businesses or Projects**: Freelancers or entrepreneurs often handle more than one project or business. A separate account for each business can help maintain clarity and organization in communications.

3. **Privacy Concerns**: Sometimes, users need a second account for privacy reasons. For instance, you might want to use a dedicated account for public interactions or online communities while keeping your personal account private.

4. **Testing and Development**: If you're a developer or a marketing professional working on campaigns that involve Viber, having multiple accounts can allow you to test features or communication strategies effectively.

Options for Managing Multiple Accounts on Viber

Viber doesn't natively allow users to run multiple accounts on the same app instance. However, there are several solutions available to manage multiple accounts effectively. These include:

1. Dual-SIM Phones and Viber Accounts

If you have a dual-SIM phone, you can easily create and manage two Viber accounts using separate phone numbers. Here's how:

- **Step 1**: Install the Viber app on your phone.

- **Step 2**: Register the first account using your primary phone number.

- **Step 3**: Use a feature like "Dual Apps" (on Android) or "App Clone" (on some devices) to install a second instance of Viber.

- **Step 4**: Register the second account using your secondary phone number.

Note: Dual-SIM functionality is only applicable if you have two active phone numbers.

2. Using Third-Party Apps or App Cloning

On devices that support app cloning, you can create a duplicate version of Viber. This cloned app functions as a separate installation, allowing you to log in with a second account.

- On Android: Use built-in features like "Dual Apps" or download third-party apps such as **Parallel Space** or **Dual Space**.

- On iOS: While app cloning is less common on iOS devices, you can use multiple devices or third-party tools (with caution).

Important: When using third-party apps, ensure they are trustworthy to protect your data and privacy.

3. Viber on Desktop as a Secondary Account

Viber allows you to use the app on both your mobile and desktop simultaneously. However, you can log in to a second account on another device or computer.

- **Step 1**: Download and install Viber on your desktop or laptop.

- **Step 2**: Register your secondary phone number as a new account.

- **Step 3**: Use the desktop app to communicate through your second account while keeping your primary account on your phone.

4. Using Multiple Devices

If you have access to multiple devices (e.g., a phone and a tablet), you can install Viber on each device with a different phone number.

Setting Up and Managing Multiple Accounts

Here's a step-by-step guide to managing multiple Viber accounts effectively:

Step 1: Decide on Your Phone Numbers

Before creating multiple accounts, ensure you have access to separate phone numbers. Each Viber account requires a unique number for registration and verification.

Step 2: Install and Register

- Install Viber on your primary device and register the first account with your main number.

- Use cloning tools or a secondary device to register the second account.

Step 3: Organize Contacts

To avoid confusion, categorize your contacts for each account. Use descriptive names, tags, or groups to identify personal and professional connections.

Step 4: Customize Notifications

Customize notification tones and settings for each account to distinguish messages and calls from one another easily.

Step 5: Sync Across Devices (Optional)

If needed, sync your accounts across devices to ensure you can access messages and calls on the go.

Best Practices for Managing Multiple Viber Accounts

Managing multiple accounts can be tricky, especially if you're handling high volumes of communication. Here are some best practices to help you stay organized:

1. **Use Clear Profile Pictures and Names**: Set unique profile pictures and names for each account to avoid sending messages from the wrong account accidentally.

2. **Schedule Account-Specific Times**: Allocate specific times for checking each account to ensure you're responsive without feeling overwhelmed.

3. **Enable Cloud Backups**: For both accounts, enable cloud backups to protect your conversations in case of accidental deletion or device loss.

4. **Log Out When Necessary**: If using a shared device for a secondary account, make sure to log out after use to maintain privacy and security.

5. **Monitor Notifications**: Turn on account-specific notifications or use silent modes when focusing on one account to reduce distractions.

Potential Challenges and How to Overcome Them

While managing multiple accounts offers flexibility, it may come with certain challenges:

1. **Switching Between Accounts**: If you need to switch accounts frequently, app cloning or using separate devices can save time.

2. **Notification Overload**: Customize notification settings to avoid being overwhelmed by constant alerts.

3. **Remembering Passwords and Numbers**: Use a secure password manager to keep track of your account credentials.

4. **Security Risks with Third-Party Apps**: Always verify the credibility of third-party tools before using them to avoid potential data breaches.

Conclusion

Managing multiple Viber accounts is an excellent way to separate your personal, professional, and other communication needs. By leveraging tools like app cloning, dual-SIM phones, or desktop apps, you can handle multiple accounts with ease while staying organized. Whether you're managing business communications or just keeping your life compartmentalized, the strategies outlined in this chapter will ensure a smooth and effective experience.

8.4 Setting Up Shortcuts and Quick Replies

Shortcuts and quick replies are invaluable tools in Viber for saving time and improving the efficiency of your communication. Whether you're managing personal conversations or juggling multiple group chats, these features ensure that you can respond faster and stay organized. In this section, we'll cover what shortcuts and quick replies are, how to set them up, and the best practices to make the most of these time-saving features.

What Are Shortcuts and Quick Replies?

Shortcuts are customizable actions that allow you to perform specific tasks in Viber with a single tap or click. They can include navigating to your most-used chats, accessing community tools, or even performing advanced actions like sending pre-drafted messages.

Quick replies, on the other hand, are pre-written messages you can send with minimal effort. Instead of typing the same response multiple times—like "I'm on my way," or "Let's connect later"—you can save these messages and access them instantly when needed.

Both features are designed to enhance productivity, making Viber especially useful for busy users who want to streamline their communication.

Setting Up Shortcuts

Shortcuts can be set up for a variety of functions within Viber. Here's how to do it step by step:

Step 1: Identify Commonly Used Actions

Before setting up shortcuts, consider which actions you perform most frequently in Viber. For example:

- Opening specific group chats or conversations.

- Starting a new call or video chat.

- Navigating to pinned messages or saved media.

Step 2: Creating Shortcuts on Mobile

1. Open the Viber app on your mobile device.

2. Navigate to **Settings** > **Shortcuts & Tools**.

3. Tap **Add Shortcut** and select the action you want to automate (e.g., open a chat, start a call).

4. Customize the shortcut's name and icon for easy recognition.

5. Save the shortcut, and it will appear on your device's home screen or as a widget, depending on your operating system.

Step 3: Setting Up Shortcuts on Desktop

1. Launch the Viber desktop application.

2. Go to the **Tools** menu and select **Keyboard Shortcuts**.

3. Assign shortcuts to actions like muting/unmuting, replying to a chat, or starting a new message.

4. Save the configuration and start using your custom shortcuts.

Setting Up Quick Replies

Quick replies are equally easy to set up, enabling you to instantly send pre-written messages with a tap or click. Follow these steps to create and use quick replies in Viber:

Step 1: Access the Quick Reply Settings

1. Open Viber and go to **Settings** > **Quick Replies**.

2. Tap **Add New Quick Reply** to start creating your message.

Step 2: Draft Your Message

- Type out the message you want to save. For example:

    o "I'll get back to you shortly."

    o "Can't talk right now, but I'll call later."

    o "Thanks for your message. Let's discuss this tomorrow."

- Keep the messages short and relevant for situations where you need a quick response.

Step 3: Save and Use Your Quick Replies

- Once you've drafted your quick reply, save it.

- To use it, simply long-press the message input field in any chat and select your saved reply from the list.

Practical Use Cases for Shortcuts and Quick Replies

1. Managing Group Chats

If you're part of multiple group chats, shortcuts can help you quickly navigate to the most active ones. Additionally, quick replies like "Noted, thanks!" or "Let's finalize this later" can be invaluable when managing professional group discussions.

2. Scheduling and Coordinating Events

Shortcuts can be set up to access Viber Communities or polls, streamlining the event planning process. Meanwhile, quick replies like "Here's the link to join" or "I'll confirm the details shortly" can save time when coordinating with multiple people.

3. Enhancing Customer Communication

For business users, quick replies can act as canned responses for frequently asked questions. For example:

- "Thank you for reaching out! We'll get back to you within 24 hours."

- "Please check our website for more details: [Insert URL]."

Shortcuts can also help navigate to business-related features like creating announcements or sharing media files.

Best Practices for Using Shortcuts and Quick Replies

1. **Keep Quick Replies Relevant**: Avoid cluttering your quick reply list with generic or outdated messages. Regularly review and update them to ensure they align with your communication needs.

2. **Use Descriptive Shortcut Names**: When setting up shortcuts, use clear and descriptive names so you can easily identify their purpose. For example, name a shortcut "Team Chat" instead of "Group 1."

3. **Prioritize Frequently Used Features**: Focus on creating shortcuts for the actions you perform most often. For instance, if you frequently video call a particular contact, prioritize setting up a shortcut for that specific action.

4. **Test and Refine**: Experiment with different shortcuts and quick replies to find what works best for you. Adjust as needed based on your habits and preferences.

Limitations and Challenges

While shortcuts and quick replies are powerful, they do have some limitations:

- **Limited Customization on Older Devices**: Certain operating systems or older versions of Viber may not support advanced shortcuts or widget-based setups.

- **Overuse of Quick Replies**: Relying too much on canned responses might make your communication feel less personal, so use them judiciously.

- **Learning Curve for New Users**: Setting up these features may seem overwhelming at first, but once familiarized, they become second nature.

Conclusion

Shortcuts and quick replies in Viber are game-changing features that enhance productivity and simplify communication. By taking the time to set them up, you can save valuable time, respond more effectively, and manage your chats with ease. Whether you're a casual user or leveraging Viber for professional purposes, these tools are sure to make your experience more seamless and efficient.

8.5 Discovering Viber Bots and Services

Viber is more than just a messaging and calling platform—it is also a hub for automation, entertainment, and productivity through the use of **Viber Bots** and **Viber Services**. This chapter explores how these features can enrich your communication experience, make your daily tasks more efficient, and even provide you with entertainment options.

What Are Viber Bots?

Viber Bots are automated tools or programs integrated within the app to assist users with specific tasks. They operate using artificial intelligence (AI) and are designed to perform a variety of functions, such as delivering news, processing orders, or answering frequently asked questions. Viber Bots are available to all users, and they're accessible through the app's interface like any other chat.

Popular Use Cases for Viber Bots

1. **Customer Support**: Businesses often use Viber Bots to offer 24/7 customer support. These bots can handle inquiries about products, troubleshoot problems, or assist with online purchases.

Example: A clothing retailer might set up a bot to help customers track orders or find sizing charts.

2. **News Updates**: Many news outlets have Viber Bots that send users breaking news updates, weather forecasts, or sports scores.

Example: Subscribe to a bot from your favorite news agency to receive daily briefings or real-time alerts.

3. **Entertainment and Games**: Some bots are designed for fun and entertainment, offering interactive quizzes, trivia games, or challenges.

Example: A movie trivia bot can provide daily questions to test your film knowledge while competing with friends.

4. **Online Shopping and Orders**: Viber Bots can facilitate online purchases, allowing you to browse products, check availability, and place orders directly through the app.

Example: A restaurant might use a bot to let customers order food, make reservations, or track delivery statuses.

5. **Educational Content**: Educational bots deliver bite-sized lessons, language learning exercises, or tips for personal development.

Example: A language-learning bot can send daily vocabulary words or short quizzes to help you practice.

How to Find and Add Viber Bots

Adding a Viber Bot to your chat list is simple:

1. **Search in the Explore Tab**: Open the Viber app and tap on the "Explore" icon. Here, you'll find a curated list of popular bots.

2. **Search by Name**: Use the search bar to find a specific bot or service by typing its name or keywords.

3. **Add and Start Chatting**: Once you find a bot you're interested in, tap "Add" to start interacting with it.

Tip: Always review a bot's description and user ratings to ensure it meets your needs and is from a trusted source.

Customizing Your Viber Bot Experience

Viber allows you to personalize your interactions with bots:

- **Notifications**: Enable or disable notifications for each bot to avoid unnecessary interruptions.

- **Unsubscribing**: If you no longer wish to use a bot, simply delete the chat or unsubscribe from its updates.

- **Blocking Bots**: If a bot sends you spam or unwanted messages, you can block it the same way you would block a user.

Exploring Viber Services

In addition to bots, Viber offers **services** that integrate seamlessly with its platform. These services provide extended functionality and are especially useful for businesses and power users.

1. **Viber Business Messages**: Businesses can send transactional messages to users, such as appointment reminders, shipping updates, or promotional offers.

2. **Public Accounts**: Brands, organizations, and influencers often use public accounts to share updates, promote campaigns, or engage with followers. Users can follow these accounts to stay informed about their favorite topics.

3. **Marketplace Services**: Viber has integrated with several third-party services, such as booking platforms, shopping apps, and payment systems, enabling you to perform these tasks without leaving the app.

Best Practices for Using Bots and Services

1. **Choose Trusted Bots**: Stick to bots from verified businesses or popular services to avoid scams. Verified bots usually have a checkmark or badge next to their name.

2. **Limit Permissions**: Some bots may request access to your data or account details. Only grant permissions that are absolutely necessary for the bot's functionality.

3. **Report Suspicious Bots**: If you encounter a bot that seems malicious or spammy, report it to Viber's support team.

4. **Stay Organized**: Too many bots can clutter your chat list. Regularly review your active bots and remove those you no longer use.

Examples of Must-Try Viber Bots

Here are some highly rated bots to explore:

- **World News Bot**: Stay updated with the latest global headlines.
- **WeatherBot**: Get accurate, real-time weather forecasts.
- **QuizMe Bot**: Test your general knowledge with fun quizzes.
- **Foodie Finder Bot**: Discover the best restaurants and recipes.
- **LanguageBot**: Learn a new language with interactive lessons.

The Future of Viber Bots and Services

The Viber team continuously enhances its bot and service ecosystem. In the future, we can expect:

1. **More AI Integration**: Advanced bots with smarter, context-aware responses.
2. **Better Customization**: Enhanced options for users to tailor bots to their preferences.
3. **Deeper Business Integration**: Businesses will leverage bots for seamless customer interactions, from product recommendations to automated billing.

Conclusion

Viber Bots and Services add a whole new dimension to the app, transforming it from a simple communication tool to a comprehensive platform for productivity, learning, and entertainment. By exploring and utilizing these features, you can enhance your Viber experience and make your everyday tasks more efficient and enjoyable.

Take the time to experiment with different bots and services—whether you're looking for fun, information, or convenience, Viber has something for everyone!

PART IV
Support and Safety

9. Troubleshooting and Support

9.1 Common Issues and How to Solve Them

As with any technology, Viber users may encounter occasional issues while using the app. From connectivity problems to account-related challenges, understanding common problems and their solutions will help you maintain a seamless experience. In this chapter, we will explore the most frequent issues faced by Viber users and provide practical solutions to overcome them.

---

1. Connectivity Issues

One of the most common problems users face is difficulty connecting to Viber services. This can manifest as messages not being sent or calls failing to connect. Connectivity problems are often linked to unstable internet connections or network restrictions.

How to Solve Connectivity Issues:

1. **Check Your Internet Connection**:

    o   Ensure that your Wi-Fi or mobile data connection is active and stable.

    o   Test your connection by visiting a website or using another app that requires the internet.

2. **Switch Networks**:

    o   If you're using Wi-Fi, try switching to mobile data, or vice versa.

    o   If the issue persists, restart your router or modem.

3. **Disable VPNs or Proxies**:

   o Some VPNs or proxy servers can interfere with Viber's functionality. Disable these services temporarily to see if it resolves the issue.

4. **Update Viber**:

   o An outdated version of Viber may cause connectivity problems. Ensure you are using the latest version of the app by checking for updates in your device's app store.

2. Account Verification Problems

When setting up Viber on a new device, users may experience issues during the account verification process, such as not receiving the SMS or call with the verification code.

How to Solve Account Verification Problems:

1. **Verify Your Phone Number**:

   o Double-check the phone number you entered to ensure it's correct.

   o Include the correct country code (e.g., +1 for the US).

2. **Wait and Retry**:

   o If you don't receive the code immediately, wait a few minutes and try again.

3. **Request a Call Instead of SMS**:

   o If the SMS doesn't arrive, select the option to receive the code via a phone call.

4. **Check Spam Filters**:

   o Ensure your mobile carrier isn't blocking messages or calls from Viber. Contact your carrier for assistance if needed.

3. Messages Not Sending or Receiving

Another frequent issue occurs when messages fail to send or are delayed. This can disrupt communication and lead to frustration.

How to Solve Messaging Issues:

1. **Confirm Your Contact's Availability**:

   o   Ensure the recipient has an active internet connection and their Viber account is functional.

2. **Clear App Cache**:

   o   On Android, go to Settings > Apps > Viber > Storage > Clear Cache.

   o   On iOS, reinstalling the app can help refresh cached data.

3. **Restart the App**:

   o   Close the app completely and reopen it to refresh its functionality.

4. **Recheck Network Settings**:

   o   As messaging relies on connectivity, ensure both your and the recipient's internet connections are stable.

---

4. Audio and Video Call Issues

Users may encounter poor call quality, dropped calls, or problems with video calls.

How to Solve Audio and Video Call Issues:

1. **Check Microphone and Camera Permissions**:

   o   Ensure Viber has permission to access your microphone and camera. Go to your device's settings to enable these permissions.

2. **Reduce Network Load**:

   o   Poor call quality often stems from bandwidth issues. Close other apps that may be consuming bandwidth.

3. **Use a Stable Internet Connection**:

   o   Video calls require a more robust connection than text messages. Switch to a stronger Wi-Fi signal if possible.

4. **Adjust Video Quality**:

    o   In Viber settings, lower the video quality to reduce lag during calls.

5. Notification Problems

Missed notifications can cause users to lose track of important messages or calls.

How to Solve Notification Issues:

1. **Enable Notifications in Viber**:

       o   Go to Viber > Settings > Notifications, and ensure all options are enabled.

2. **Check Device Notification Settings**:

       o   On your phone, ensure notifications for Viber are not muted or disabled.

3. **Disable Do Not Disturb Mode**:

       o   If your device is in "Do Not Disturb" mode, you won't receive notifications. Disable this mode or add Viber as an exception.

4. **Battery Optimization Settings**:

       o   On Android, battery optimization may restrict Viber from running in the background. Go to Settings > Battery > Battery Optimization, and exclude Viber.

6. App Crashes or Freezes

If Viber crashes or freezes frequently, it can interrupt your usage and lead to frustration.

How to Solve App Crashes or Freezing Issues:

1. **Update the App**:

       o   Ensure you have the latest version of Viber installed. Updates often include bug fixes and performance improvements.

2. **Restart Your Device**:

       o   A simple restart can resolve temporary glitches.

3. **Clear Cache and Data**:

- o On Android, clear the app cache as explained earlier. If the issue persists, clear app data (this will log you out, so ensure your account is backed up).

4. **Reinstall Viber**:

- o Uninstall the app and download it again from the official app store.

---

7. Contact Syncing Issues

Sometimes, Viber may not sync all of your contacts or show incorrect names.

How to Solve Contact Syncing Issues:

1. **Refresh Contacts in Viber**:

- o Go to Viber > Settings > Privacy > Contacts and tap "Sync Contacts."

2. **Check Device Permissions**:

- o Ensure Viber has permission to access your phone's contacts.

3. **Manually Add Contacts**:

- o If a contact doesn't appear, add them manually by entering their phone number into Viber.

---

8. Backup and Restore Issues

If you lose chats or cannot restore a backup, it can be distressing, especially if the data is important.

How to Solve Backup and Restore Issues:

1. **Verify Backup Settings**:

- o Ensure your Viber backup is enabled and linked to Google Drive (Android) or iCloud (iOS).

2. **Check Available Storage**:

- o Ensure there is enough storage in your Google Drive or iCloud account to save the backup.

3. **Restore Correct Backup**:

   o When restoring, ensure you're logged into the same Google/iCloud account used for the backup.

9. Error Messages

Users may occasionally see generic error messages like "Something went wrong."

How to Solve Error Messages:

1. **Restart the App**:

   o Close and reopen Viber.

2. **Clear Cache and Update**:

   o Clear the app cache and check for updates.

3. **Contact Viber Support**:

   o If the error persists, reach out to Viber support through the app or their website.

By addressing these common issues with practical solutions, you can ensure a smooth and hassle-free experience with Viber. For more persistent or uncommon problems, the next section provides guidance on contacting Viber support and staying updated with the app's latest features.

9.2 Contacting Viber Support

When you encounter issues with Viber that you can't solve on your own, contacting Viber Support is often the best course of action. The team at Viber Support is equipped to help users resolve technical problems, answer questions, and provide guidance on using the platform effectively. In this section, we'll explore the various ways you can contact Viber Support, best practices for ensuring a quick resolution, and some helpful tips to make the process as smooth as possible.

1. Understanding Viber's Support Channels

Viber offers several ways for users to seek help and report issues. The primary support channels include:

1.1 In-App Help Center

Viber has an integrated Help Center that provides quick answers to common questions. This is often the fastest way to get help for minor issues without needing to contact a support representative.

- To access the Help Center, open the Viber app, go to the **More** tab, and select **Help & Support**.

- Browse through categories such as "Getting Started," "Messaging," "Calling," or "Account Issues" to find detailed guides and FAQs.

- Use the search bar to find specific topics.

1.2 Online Support Portal

If the in-app Help Center doesn't solve your problem, the next step is to visit Viber's official support website at support.viber.com.

- The online portal offers a more comprehensive database of articles and troubleshooting guides.

- You can search for specific issues, such as "connection problems" or "payment issues," and follow step-by-step instructions to resolve them.

1.3 Submitting a Support Request

For complex or unresolved issues, submitting a support request allows you to get personalized assistance from the Viber Support team.

- On the online portal, select the **Contact Us** button.

- Fill out the support form with the following details:

    o **Your email address** (used for correspondence).

    o **Category of your issue** (e.g., technical problem, payment inquiry, account recovery).

○ **A detailed description** of the issue, including any error messages or steps that caused the problem.

○ **Attachments** (screenshots or logs) to provide visual evidence of the issue.

- Once submitted, you'll receive a confirmation email with a ticket number for tracking your case.

1.4 Social Media Channels

Viber's official social media accounts are another way to seek help. While these are not meant for in-depth technical support, you can use them to ask general questions or report major outages.

- Twitter: @Viber

- Facebook: Viber's official page

2. Preparing for Contacting Viber Support

To get the best results when reaching out to Viber Support, it's important to prepare the necessary information. This ensures that the support team has everything they need to diagnose and solve your issue efficiently.

2.1 Key Information to Include

- **Your Viber Phone Number:** Ensure you provide the correct phone number linked to your Viber account.

- **Device Details:** Include your device's make, model, and operating system version (e.g., iPhone 13 running iOS 16 or Samsung Galaxy S21 with Android 12).

- **App Version:** Mention the version of the Viber app you're using. You can find this in the app under **Settings > About**.

- **Detailed Issue Description:** Clearly explain what happened, when it started, and any actions you've already taken to try and fix the problem.

- **Screenshots or Error Messages:** Attach images or descriptions of error messages, as they provide critical clues for troubleshooting.

2.2 Be Clear and Concise

When describing your issue, avoid vague terms like "It doesn't work." Instead, use clear and specific language such as:

- "The app crashes every time I try to open a group chat."

- "I am unable to make calls; the error message says, 'No Internet connection,' but my Wi-Fi is working."

2.3 Check for Known Issues

Before contacting support, check Viber's official website or social media channels for announcements about known issues. Sometimes, widespread problems (e.g., server outages) are already being addressed, and you won't need to submit a support ticket.

3. Best Practices for Faster Resolution

3.1 Use the Right Support Category

When submitting a support request, selecting the correct category is crucial. For example:

- **Account Recovery:** If you've lost access to your account or need to change your phone number.

- **Technical Problems:** For issues like app crashes, call quality, or missing messages.

- **Payment Inquiries:** For problems with Viber Out credit or subscription renewals.

3.2 Respond Promptly

Once you've submitted a request, Viber Support may reply with follow-up questions or additional instructions. Responding quickly helps resolve your issue faster.

3.3 Keep Track of Your Ticket Number

When you submit a support request, you'll receive a ticket number. Save this number for future reference if you need to follow up on your case.

4. Common Scenarios Requiring Support

4.1 Account-Related Issues

- **Lost Access to Account:** If you've changed your phone number or lost your device, Viber Support can help you recover your account.

- **Verification Problems:** For issues with receiving verification codes, ensure you have a stable internet connection and correct phone number format.

4.2 Connection and Call Quality Problems

- **Low Call Quality:** Support can guide you through improving call performance by checking your internet connection or adjusting app settings.

- **Connection Drops:** If calls or messages fail due to connectivity issues, you may receive instructions for optimizing your device settings.

4.3 Payment and Subscription Issues

- **Viber Out Credit Problems:** For inquiries about Viber Out credits not appearing after purchase, attach proof of payment to your support request.

- **Subscription Renewal Errors:** Contact support if your subscription isn't renewed despite automatic payment being enabled.

---

5. When to Expect a Response

Viber Support typically responds within 24 to 48 hours, though response times may vary depending on the complexity of the issue and the volume of support requests. During peak periods, such as app updates or global outages, expect slightly longer wait times.

Tips While Waiting:

- Check your spam or junk email folder for responses.

- Avoid submitting multiple tickets for the same issue, as this can delay resolution.

---

6. Staying Updated with Viber

To prevent issues and stay informed about new features or updates, regularly check Viber's:

- **Official Blog** for announcements and feature releases.

- **Social Media Channels** for real-time updates about outages or maintenance.

- **App Updates** to ensure you're running the latest version with bug fixes and improvements.

By understanding how to contact Viber Support effectively, you can ensure that your issues are addressed quickly and efficiently. Whether you're dealing with account recovery, technical glitches, or payment concerns, the support team is there to help you stay connected without interruption.

9.3 Staying Updated with New Features

Staying updated with the latest features of Viber is essential to maximize its functionality and take full advantage of its evolving capabilities. In this section, we'll explore the importance of keeping Viber up-to-date, how to ensure you're always running the latest version, and how to discover and utilize newly released features to enhance your experience.

The Importance of Staying Updated

Technology evolves rapidly, and apps like Viber are no exception. Regular updates provide several key benefits:

1. **Improved Security:** Updates often address vulnerabilities and enhance the app's encryption standards, ensuring your conversations remain private and secure.

2. **Bug Fixes:** Developers continuously work to resolve bugs or glitches that users encounter. Keeping Viber updated ensures smoother performance.

3. **Access to New Features:** Updates introduce innovative features that enhance usability, like improved group call options or enhanced sticker management tools.

4. **Compatibility with Devices:** Newer versions of operating systems on phones and computers may require updated apps for compatibility, preventing crashes or limited functionality.

Neglecting updates can lead to missed opportunities, reduced security, and potential technical issues.

How to Keep Viber Updated

Automatic Updates

Most smartphones allow you to enable automatic updates for apps, including Viber. This feature ensures that updates are downloaded and installed without requiring manual intervention. To enable automatic updates:

- **On Android:**

    1. Open the **Google Play Store**.

    2. Tap your profile icon in the top-right corner.

    3. Go to **Settings > Network Preferences > Auto-update apps**.

    4. Choose **Over any network** or **Over Wi-Fi only** to save data.

- **On iOS:**

    1. Open **Settings** on your iPhone.

    2. Scroll down and tap **App Store**.

    3. Toggle on **App Updates** under **Automatic Downloads**.

Manual Updates

If you prefer to control when updates occur, you can manually update Viber:

- Open the **Google Play Store** (Android) or **App Store** (iOS).

- Search for "Viber."

- If an update is available, the button will display **Update** instead of **Open**. Tap it to install the latest version.

Discovering New Features

Each update often comes with new tools, enhancements, or design changes that can improve your experience. Here's how you can stay informed about what's new:

Release Notes

When you update Viber, app stores typically provide release notes that summarize the new features and fixes. Make it a habit to skim these notes to learn about changes and additions.

In-App Notifications

Viber frequently announces new features through in-app messages or banners. These notifications may appear at the top of your chats or in the settings menu.

Viber Blog and Website

Visit the official **Viber blog** or website to read detailed articles about the latest updates. The blog often includes screenshots, tutorials, and tips on using new features.

Social Media Channels

Follow Viber on social media platforms like Facebook, Twitter, and Instagram. These channels are regularly updated with news, feature announcements, and promotional content.

Community Forums

Engaging with the Viber community on forums or discussion groups allows you to learn from other users who may already be exploring new features.

Exploring New Features

When a new feature is introduced, it's essential to experiment and explore its functionality. Here are some examples of recent Viber features and how you can utilize them:

Enhanced Group Video Calls

Viber's updates have focused on making group video calls more dynamic, with features like screen sharing or live reactions. To use this feature:

1. Open a group chat and tap the video icon to start a video call.

2. Explore options like muting participants, sharing your screen, or enabling gallery view for better visuals.

Disappearing Messages

Viber now allows users to send disappearing messages for added privacy. This feature can be accessed in one-on-one chats:

1. Open a chat.

2. Tap the clock icon in the message bar to set a time limit for messages to disappear after being read.

Improved Sticker Store

The updated sticker store makes it easier to find and download free or premium sticker packs. To explore:

1. Tap the **Sticker** icon in a chat.

2. Browse categories or use the search bar to find specific stickers.

Maximizing Your Viber Experience

Staying updated isn't just about downloading the latest version; it's also about integrating new features into your daily use:

1. **Experiment and Practice:** After an update, take time to explore new features. Practice using them in conversations or test them with friends.

2. **Seek Tutorials:** Watch tutorial videos on platforms like YouTube to learn how to use complex features like Viber Communities or advanced call options.

3. **Provide Feedback:** If you encounter any issues or have suggestions for improvements, use the **Contact Support** feature to share your thoughts with Viber's developers.

Troubleshooting Update Issues

If you encounter problems updating Viber, try the following solutions:

Insufficient Storage Space

Make sure your device has enough free storage to accommodate updates. Clear unnecessary files or uninstall unused apps to create space.

Connectivity Issues

A weak or unstable internet connection can prevent updates from downloading. Connect to a reliable Wi-Fi network before attempting the update again.

App Store Glitches

If the app store isn't showing the update, try clearing the store's cache (Android) or restarting your device.

Outdated Operating System

Ensure your device's operating system is up-to-date, as older versions may not support the latest Viber updates.

Conclusion

Staying updated with new features is a crucial aspect of enjoying a seamless Viber experience. By enabling automatic updates, exploring new tools, and engaging with Viber's announcements, you can ensure that your messaging and calling remain efficient, secure, and fun. Regular updates not only enhance usability but also protect your privacy and expand the app's capabilities.

Remember, Viber isn't just a messaging app—it's a platform for connection, creativity, and communication. By staying current, you can unlock its full potential and enjoy the best it has to offer.

10. Staying Safe on Viber

10.1 Identifying and Avoiding Scams

In today's digital age, scams are becoming increasingly sophisticated, targeting unsuspecting users across all platforms, including Viber. As a communication app with millions of users worldwide, Viber offers a secure environment with end-to-end encryption. However, no platform is entirely immune to scams. This section will guide you through the common types of scams on Viber, how to identify them, and the best practices to stay safe.

Understanding Scams on Viber

Scams on Viber often involve fraudulent messages, malicious links, or fake profiles attempting to deceive users for financial gain, personal information, or account access. Knowing how these scams operate is the first step to protecting yourself.

1. Phishing Scams

Phishing is one of the most common scams on Viber. Scammers send messages pretending to be legitimate organizations, such as banks, delivery services, or even Viber itself. These messages often contain urgent language, such as:

- "Your account has been compromised. Click here to secure it."

- "You have won a prize! Claim it now."

When users click on the provided link, they are directed to a fake website designed to steal their login credentials, personal details, or payment information.

2. Fake Promotions or Giveaways

Scammers frequently use fake promotions or giveaways to lure users. Messages like "Congratulations! You've won a free phone. Click here to claim your prize" are designed to trick users into providing sensitive information or making payments to claim the supposed reward.

3. Malicious Links

Messages containing links to external websites can sometimes lead to malware downloads or phishing sites. These links might appear to come from a trusted contact whose account has been compromised.

4. Impersonation Scams

Scammers may create fake profiles that mimic a person you know, a celebrity, or a representative from an organization. Once trust is established, they may request money, sensitive information, or ask you to download a malicious file.

5. Financial Scams

Scammers may pretend to be someone in financial distress or offer fake investment opportunities. These scams often play on emotions or promise quick and high returns on investments.

6. OTP (One-Time Password) Scams

Some scammers request users to share their One-Time Password (OTP), which is sent via SMS or Viber. This can lead to account hijacking if the OTP is provided.

How to Identify Scams on Viber

Recognizing the warning signs of scams can save you from falling victim. Here are some key red flags:

1. Unsolicited Messages

If you receive a message from someone you don't know or weren't expecting, proceed with caution. Genuine contacts or companies rarely send random messages without prior interaction.

2. Requests for Sensitive Information

Legitimate organizations will never ask for passwords, OTPs, or bank details via Viber messages. Be skeptical of any message requesting such information.

3. Poor Grammar and Spelling

Many scam messages contain noticeable grammar and spelling errors. This is often a sign of fraudulent activity.

4. Urgency and Pressure

Scammers often use time-sensitive language to pressure you into acting quickly without thinking. Phrases like "Act now" or "Offer expires in 24 hours" are commonly used.

5. Suspicious Links

Hover over any links in messages (if possible) and check if the URL matches the sender's claims. Avoid clicking on links you don't trust.

6. Too Good to Be True Offers

If a message claims you've won a prize, received a large sum of money, or are eligible for an exclusive deal, question its authenticity.

7. Profile Authenticity

Check the sender's profile picture, name, and activity. Scammers often use generic names, fake photos, or recently created accounts.

How to Avoid Scams on Viber

Being proactive is the best way to stay safe. Here are practical tips to avoid falling victim to scams on Viber:

1. Verify the Sender's Identity

If you receive a suspicious message, verify the sender's identity by contacting them directly through a trusted channel. Do not rely solely on the information provided in the message.

2. Avoid Clicking on Suspicious Links

Even if a message appears to come from a trusted source, avoid clicking on links unless you are certain of their authenticity. Use a secure browser to inspect links if needed.

3. Never Share Sensitive Information

Do not share your passwords, OTPs, or personal details with anyone, even if the request seems legitimate.

4. Enable Privacy Settings

Viber offers various privacy settings to protect your account. You can:

- Restrict who can see your profile photo.

- Hide your online status.

- Limit who can add you to groups.

5. Use Two-Step Verification

Enable two-step verification to add an extra layer of security to your Viber account. This requires a PIN in addition to your password when logging in.

6. Block and Report Scammers

If you encounter a suspicious account, block and report it immediately. Viber's team will investigate and take necessary action.

7. Keep Your App Updated

Always use the latest version of Viber. Updates often include security patches that protect against new threats.

8. Educate Yourself

Stay informed about the latest scams and how they operate. Knowledge is your best defense.

What to Do If You've Been Scammed

If you suspect you've fallen victim to a scam, take immediate action:

1. Change Your Password

If your account may have been compromised, change your Viber password immediately.

2. Enable Two-Step Verification

Add two-step verification to prevent unauthorized access.

3. Report the Scam

Use Viber's built-in reporting feature to notify the platform about the scam.

4. Notify Relevant Authorities

If you've lost money or personal information, report the incident to local authorities or a cybercrime unit.

5. Monitor Your Accounts

Keep an eye on your bank accounts, email, and other sensitive platforms for any suspicious activity.

Conclusion

Staying safe on Viber requires vigilance and awareness. By learning to identify scams, practicing caution, and using the platform's privacy features, you can enjoy a secure and seamless communication experience. Remember, if something seems suspicious, trust your instincts and verify before acting.

10.2 Using Two-Step Verification

Two-step verification (2SV) is a powerful tool to protect your Viber account from unauthorized access and ensure that your personal data remains secure. In this chapter, we'll explore everything you need to know about enabling, using, and managing two-step verification on Viber. Whether you're a casual user or rely on Viber for business communications, implementing this security feature is crucial in today's digital world.

What Is Two-Step Verification?

Two-step verification is an added layer of security for your Viber account. It requires a second form of authentication, typically a unique PIN code, in addition to your phone number. This prevents unauthorized access even if someone else has your phone number or SIM card.

By enabling 2SV, you're effectively creating a digital lock that only you can open, making it nearly impossible for hackers to access your account without the PIN.

Why Is Two-Step Verification Important?

1. **Protecting Your Personal Information**: Viber stores your chats, contacts, media files, and call history. If someone gains access to your account, they could misuse

this information, compromising your privacy. Two-step verification ensures your account remains private.

2. **Preventing Account Takeovers**: Cybercriminals often target messaging apps to hijack accounts. With two-step verification, even if they have your phone number, they can't access your account without the PIN you've set.

3. **Securing Sensitive Conversations**: If you use Viber for work or share sensitive information, two-step verification adds an extra layer of protection, ensuring that confidential data doesn't fall into the wrong hands.

How to Enable Two-Step Verification on Viber

Enabling two-step verification on Viber is straightforward. Follow these steps to secure your account:

1. **Open Viber**

    o Launch the Viber app on your smartphone. Ensure you're using the latest version for optimal security.

2. **Go to Settings**

    o Tap on the three horizontal lines or the **More** option (depending on your device) at the bottom right of the app.

    o Select **Settings** from the menu.

3. **Navigate to Privacy**

    o In the **Settings** menu, tap on **Privacy**.

4. **Select Two-Step Verification**

    o Look for the **Two-Step Verification** option and tap on it.

5. **Set Your PIN**

    o You'll be prompted to create a six-digit PIN. Choose a number that's easy for you to remember but hard for others to guess. Avoid using common sequences like "123456" or your birth year.

6. **Enter Your Email Address**

o Viber may ask for an email address as a backup. This is crucial if you forget your PIN. Make sure the email address is valid and one you regularly check.

7. **Confirm Your Email and PIN**

o Viber will send a confirmation email to the address you provided. Open the email and follow the instructions to complete the setup.

Best Practices for Using Two-Step Verification

1. **Choose a Strong PIN**

o Avoid predictable numbers like birthdays or repetitive digits. A strong PIN could be a mix of memorable but unique numbers.

2. **Keep Your Email Secure**

o Since your email is used as a backup for two-step verification, ensure it's secure with its own strong password and two-factor authentication (if available).

3. **Don't Share Your PIN**

o Never share your PIN with anyone, even if they claim to be from Viber support. Legitimate Viber representatives will never ask for your PIN.

4. **Update Your Email Regularly**

o If you change your primary email address, update it in Viber to avoid losing access to your account in case you forget your PIN.

5. **Be Cautious with Public Devices**

o Avoid entering your PIN on shared or public devices. These devices may have malware that can capture your credentials.

What Happens If You Forget Your PIN?

Forgetting your PIN doesn't mean losing access to your account forever. Here's what you can do:

1. **Reset via Email**

- o During the two-step verification setup, you provided a backup email. If you forget your PIN, Viber will allow you to reset it using this email.

2. **Request a PIN Reset**

- o Open Viber, navigate to the two-step verification page, and tap on the option to reset your PIN. Follow the instructions sent to your email to set a new PIN.

3. **Reinstall Viber**

- o As a last resort, you can uninstall and reinstall Viber. Keep in mind that this will log you out of all devices, and you'll need to re-verify your phone number to access your account again.

Common Issues and Solutions

1. **Forgotten Email Address**

- o If you forget the email address you used for two-step verification, contact Viber Support. Provide any relevant details, such as your phone number and account activity, to verify your identity.

2. **PIN Reset Not Working**

- o Ensure you're checking the correct email inbox (including the spam folder). If you still don't receive the reset email, try again later or contact support.

3. **Frequent PIN Prompts**

- o Viber may ask for your PIN more frequently if you log in on multiple devices. To minimize this, ensure you're using the app only on trusted devices.

Benefits of Two-Step Verification for Businesses

For businesses using Viber for customer communication or team collaboration, two-step verification is essential for protecting sensitive data, such as customer inquiries, marketing plans, or financial details. Here's why it's a must:

1. **Builds Customer Trust**

    o   A secure account reduces the risk of data breaches, helping to build trust with your customers.

2. **Protects Business Assets**

    o   Safeguard your contacts, conversations, and shared files from unauthorized access.

3. **Ensures Compliance**

    o   Many industries require secure communication channels. Two-step verification helps ensure compliance with data protection regulations.

Final Thoughts

Two-step verification is an essential tool for anyone who values their privacy and security on Viber. By taking a few minutes to enable this feature, you can significantly reduce the risk of unauthorized access and protect your personal or business data.

Make it a priority to enable two-step verification today. Your Viber account—and the information it holds—deserves nothing less.

10.3 Maintaining Online Etiquette

Maintaining proper online etiquette, also known as "netiquette," is essential when using any communication platform, including Viber. Good online manners not only foster positive interactions but also protect your privacy and ensure a respectful experience for everyone involved. In this section, we'll explore key principles of maintaining online etiquette on Viber, practical tips for handling different situations, and how adhering to these practices enhances your overall experience on the platform.

What is Online Etiquette?

Online etiquette refers to the polite and respectful behavior expected in digital interactions. On Viber, where users engage in personal chats, group discussions, or even professional communications, netiquette is crucial to ensure smooth and enjoyable conversations. Poor etiquette can lead to misunderstandings, conflict, or even being blocked by other users.

Good online etiquette on Viber encompasses the following:

- Respect for others' time and privacy.

- Clear and concise communication.

- Responsible use of group chats and communities.

- Sensitivity toward different cultures and opinions.

By understanding and practicing these principles, you'll not only communicate effectively but also build stronger and more respectful relationships.

Key Principles of Online Etiquette on Viber

1. Respect Privacy and Boundaries

- **Seek Permission Before Calling:** Avoid making unsolicited calls, especially video calls. Not everyone may be available or comfortable answering unexpected calls. A quick text asking, "Is this a good time to call?" can go a long way.

- **Avoid Over-Messaging:** Sending too many messages or spamming someone's inbox can be overwhelming. Respect the recipient's time by keeping your communication concise and to the point.

- **Think Before Forwarding Messages:** Before forwarding a message, ensure it's appropriate for the recipient. Avoid sharing sensitive or private information without consent.

2. Be Mindful in Group Chats

- **Stay Relevant:** When participating in group chats, keep your messages relevant to the group's purpose. For example, avoid sharing unrelated memes or personal topics in a professional group.

- **Avoid Overloading the Group:** Limit excessive notifications by refraining from sending consecutive messages or using multiple emojis unnecessarily.

- **Be Inclusive:** Ensure your contributions to group discussions are inclusive and respectful of diverse viewpoints.

3. Practice Clear Communication

- **Use Emojis and Stickers Appropriately:** Emojis and stickers can add fun to conversations but overusing them might dilute the meaning of your message. Stick to simple and relevant visuals to enhance communication.

- **Avoid Ambiguity:** Use proper grammar and punctuation to ensure your message is clear. Misunderstandings often occur due to poorly written or vague texts.

- **Check Tone and Context:** In text communication, tone can be easily misinterpreted. Use polite language and context clues to convey the intended tone, and avoid using all caps as it may be perceived as shouting.

4. Avoid Spreading False Information

- **Verify Before Sharing:** Before forwarding a news article, link, or other information, check its authenticity. Spreading fake news or misinformation can lead to panic and harm your credibility.

- **Report Harmful Content:** If you encounter spam or inappropriate material in group chats or communities, report it to the group admin or use Viber's reporting tools.

5. Show Appreciation and Courtesy

- **Say "Thank You" and "Please":** Simple courtesies can go a long way in building rapport. Acknowledge the efforts of others in group chats or thank them for their time and input.

- **Respond Promptly:** While instant replies may not always be possible, try to respond within a reasonable timeframe to maintain good communication.

Practical Scenarios and How to Handle Them

Scenario 1: Managing Conflicts in Group Chats

Group chats with diverse participants may lead to disagreements. If a conflict arises:

- Avoid escalating the situation by staying calm and respectful.

- Acknowledge differing opinions and encourage constructive dialogue.

- If the conversation becomes disruptive, suggest moving the discussion to a private chat or involve the group admin to mediate.

Scenario 2: Dealing with Unwanted Messages

If you receive unsolicited or inappropriate messages:

- Politely inform the sender that their messages are unwelcome.

- If the behavior continues, use Viber's "Block" feature to prevent further contact.

- Report the sender to Viber if the messages violate community standards.

Scenario 3: Handling Sensitive Topics

When discussing sensitive topics such as politics, religion, or personal matters:

- Avoid making assumptions about others' beliefs or opinions.

- Frame your messages in a way that invites discussion rather than argument.

- Respect others' boundaries if they choose not to engage.

Benefits of Maintaining Online Etiquette on Viber

Adhering to proper online etiquette offers numerous benefits, including:

- **Enhanced Relationships:** Respectful and thoughtful communication strengthens bonds with friends, family, and colleagues.

- **Positive Reputation:** Your online behavior reflects your character. Practicing good etiquette builds trust and respect.

- **Reduced Misunderstandings:** Clear and concise messages minimize the risk of misinterpretation.

- **Better Group Dynamics:** Responsible participation in group chats fosters a collaborative and supportive environment.

Quick Tips for Practicing Online Etiquette on Viber

1. Use the "Do Not Disturb" mode to avoid interruptions during important moments.

2. Double-check messages before sending to ensure clarity and relevance.

3. Avoid adding people to groups without their permission.

4. Apologize if you make a mistake, such as sending a message to the wrong recipient.

5. Familiarize yourself with Viber's privacy and reporting tools to address any issues proactively.

Conclusion

Maintaining online etiquette on Viber is about more than just following rules—it's about fostering meaningful and respectful connections in a digital world. By respecting others' privacy, communicating clearly, and handling conflicts gracefully, you can create a positive experience for yourself and everyone you interact with on Viber.

Practicing these principles doesn't just improve your interactions on Viber but also contributes to a healthier and more courteous online community overall.

Conclusion

11.1 Why Viber is the Best Choice for Messaging and Calls

In the ever-growing world of communication apps, Viber has emerged as a standout platform, offering an unparalleled combination of features, ease of use, and accessibility. This chapter dives deep into why Viber is the go-to choice for messaging and calls, exploring its unique capabilities, user-friendly design, and the many ways it enhances your ability to connect with others around the globe.

1. A Comprehensive Communication Platform

One of Viber's greatest strengths is its versatility. Unlike many communication apps that focus exclusively on either messaging or calling, Viber excels in both areas, providing a comprehensive platform for all your communication needs. Whether you're sending a quick text, participating in a group chat, or making a high-definition video call, Viber ensures seamless communication without compromising quality.

Messaging Features:

- **Rich Text Options:** Viber allows you to express yourself through text with a variety of options like bold, italic, and strikethrough formatting.

- **Stickers and GIFs:** With thousands of fun and expressive stickers, you can enhance your messages and bring conversations to life.

- **File Sharing:** Viber enables you to share photos, videos, and files of various formats with ease, making it ideal for both personal and professional use.

Calling Features:

- **Crystal-Clear Audio and Video Calls:** Viber's high-definition audio and video call quality make it a reliable choice, even on slower internet connections.

- **Group Calls:** Host voice or video calls with multiple participants, perfect for family catch-ups or team meetings.

- **Viber Out:** The ability to call non-Viber users at affordable rates ensures you're never disconnected, regardless of whether the other person uses the app.

2. End-to-End Encryption for Maximum Privacy

Privacy is a major concern for users of communication apps, and Viber stands out as one of the most secure platforms available. Every message, call, photo, and video shared through Viber is protected with end-to-end encryption, ensuring that only you and the intended recipient have access to the content.

Security Features:

- **Private Chats:** Viber offers hidden chats that require a PIN to access, providing an additional layer of privacy for sensitive conversations.

- **Self-Destructing Messages:** Users can send messages that disappear after a specified time, giving you full control over the content you share.

- **No Data Tracking:** Unlike some other platforms, Viber does not track or store your communication data for advertising purposes, making it a truly private option.

3. User-Friendly Interface

One of the reasons Viber is so popular is its intuitive design. Whether you're a tech-savvy millennial or a senior trying out messaging apps for the first time, Viber's interface is designed to be accessible and easy to navigate.

Key Design Highlights:

- **Simple Navigation:** Viber organizes your chats, calls, and settings into clear categories, ensuring you can quickly find what you need.

- **Customizable Themes:** Personalize your experience by choosing from a range of themes and chat backgrounds.

- **Cross-Device Syncing:** Whether you're on your phone, tablet, or desktop, Viber keeps your conversations synced across devices, allowing for seamless transitions.

4. Global Connectivity

Viber is not limited by borders. Its global presence makes it one of the most accessible communication platforms in the world. With support for over 40 languages and an expansive network of users, Viber is ideal for keeping in touch with friends, family, and colleagues no matter where they are.

Features Supporting Global Use:

- **Free International Calls:** Viber-to-Viber calls are completely free, enabling you to connect with loved ones abroad without worrying about costs.

- **Affordable Rates with Viber Out:** For non-Viber users, Viber Out offers competitive rates for international calls.

- **Language Support:** The app is available in multiple languages, making it easy for users from different parts of the world to navigate and use.

5. Innovative Features

Viber continually innovates to stay ahead of the competition, introducing features that enhance communication in unique ways.

Standout Innovations:

- **Communities:** Viber's community feature allows users to create and join large groups with unlimited members, making it perfect for fan clubs, organizations, and interest groups.

- **Polls and Surveys:** In group chats, users can create polls to quickly gather opinions or make decisions collectively.

- **Chat Extensions:** These allow you to integrate external services like YouTube, Spotify, and Giphy directly into your chats for a more dynamic experience.

6. Cost-Effectiveness

In addition to being feature-rich, Viber is also incredibly cost-effective. The app itself is free to download and use for messaging and calling other Viber users. For those who need to connect with people outside the platform, Viber Out offers rates that are significantly cheaper than traditional phone carriers.

Cost-Saving Features:

- **Free Messaging and Calls:** All Viber-to-Viber communication is free, including messages, calls, and file sharing.

- **Affordable International Calls:** Viber Out offers prepaid plans and pay-as-you-go options, ensuring affordability for all users.

7. Suitable for Both Personal and Professional Use

While Viber is widely used for personal communication, its features also make it a strong contender for professional purposes. From conducting team calls to sharing project files, Viber provides tools that are versatile enough to support work-related needs.

Professional Applications:

- **Group Collaboration:** Teams can use Viber group chats to discuss projects, share updates, and brainstorm ideas.

- **File Sharing:** The ability to send large files directly through the app simplifies collaboration.

- **Secure Communication:** Viber's robust security features ensure that sensitive work conversations remain private.

8. Continuous Updates and Improvements

Viber's development team is dedicated to improving the platform through regular updates. New features, enhanced security measures, and bug fixes are rolled out frequently to ensure the app remains competitive and reliable.

9. A Community-Oriented Platform

Unlike many communication apps, Viber fosters a sense of community among its users. Whether through public Viber Communities or customer support that listens to feedback, the platform ensures that users feel valued and connected.

Community Features:

- **Public Accounts:** Follow your favorite brands, celebrities, and organizations on Viber for exclusive updates.

- **Feedback-Friendly Development:** Viber actively listens to user suggestions and incorporates feedback into app improvements.

Conclusion

Viber's extensive feature set, commitment to privacy, and user-friendly design make it a standout choice in the crowded world of communication apps. Whether you're connecting with loved ones, collaborating with colleagues, or simply exploring its rich array of features, Viber ensures that communication is seamless, secure, and enjoyable. Choosing Viber isn't just about downloading another app; it's about embracing a smarter, more connected way to communicate.

Appendices

A. Viber Keyboard Shortcuts

Welcome**A. Viber Keyboard Shortcuts**

Keyboard shortcuts can greatly improve your productivity when using Viber, especially if you frequently use the desktop version of the application. Whether you're managing conversations, initiating calls, or customizing settings, knowing these shortcuts will help you navigate through Viber faster and with greater ease. Below is a comprehensive guide to the most useful keyboard shortcuts available in Viber, along with tips on how to integrate them into your workflow.

1. What Are Keyboard Shortcuts in Viber?

Keyboard shortcuts are predefined combinations of keys that execute specific actions within Viber without the need for mouse clicks. For example, instead of manually clicking on a chat to search for a keyword, you can use a shortcut to open the search bar instantly. These shortcuts are especially useful for professionals or heavy users of Viber who want to streamline their communication tasks.

2. Benefits of Using Keyboard Shortcuts in Viber

- **Increased Efficiency**: Quickly perform actions like opening chats, starting calls, or searching messages.

- **Ease of Multitasking**: Switch between tasks without leaving the keyboard.

- **Enhanced Accessibility**: Shortcuts make it easier for users who rely on keyboards rather than mice.

- **Professional Communication**: Faster navigation lets you focus more on conversations rather than figuring out the interface.

3. Commonly Used Keyboard Shortcuts in Viber

Here's a list of essential keyboard shortcuts for Viber Desktop, categorized by function:

Messaging and Chats

- **Ctrl + F**: Open the search bar to find keywords within a chat.
- **Ctrl + N**: Start a new conversation.
- **Ctrl + E**: Archive the current chat.
- **Ctrl + Shift + A**: Access all unread messages in one place.
- **Ctrl + Shift + L**: Pin or unpin a chat to the top of your chat list.
- **Esc**: Close the currently opened chat or window.

Calling Features

- **Ctrl + Shift + C**: Start a voice call with the selected contact.
- **Ctrl + Shift + V**: Start a video call with the selected contact.
- **Ctrl + H**: Mute or unmute the microphone during a call.
- **Ctrl + Shift + M**: Switch between audio and video modes in an active call.
- **Alt + D**: End the current call.

Navigation and Windows Management

- **Ctrl + Tab**: Switch between open conversations.
- **Ctrl + Shift + Tab**: Navigate backward between open conversations.
- **Ctrl + 1, 2, 3, etc.**: Quickly jump to a specific chat based on its position in the chat list.
- **Alt + Enter**: Toggle full-screen mode for Viber.
- **Ctrl + W**: Close the current Viber window.

Media and Attachments

- **Ctrl + O**: Open the file selection dialog to attach files to a chat.

- **Ctrl + P**: Take and send a screenshot directly in a chat.

- **Ctrl + Shift + U**: Upload a video to share with the current chat.

- **Ctrl + D**: Delete a selected photo, video, or file from a chat.

Customization and Settings

- **Ctrl + , (Comma)**: Open the Viber settings menu.

- **Ctrl + Shift + S**: Change your current status (Online, Away, Busy, etc.).

- **Ctrl + Alt + S**: Open your sticker menu to browse and send stickers.

- **Ctrl + Shift + N**: Create a new group chat.

4. How to Memorize Keyboard Shortcuts

Learning all the shortcuts at once might feel overwhelming. Here are some tips to help you gradually integrate them into your daily Viber usage:

1. **Start Small**: Begin with 2-3 shortcuts that are most relevant to your usage, such as Ctrl + F (search) and Ctrl + N (new chat).

2. **Use Visual Reminders**: Write down shortcuts on a sticky note and place it near your computer screen.

3. **Practice Daily**: The more you use shortcuts, the faster they will become second nature.

4. **Explore the Help Menu**: Viber's desktop app includes a help section where you can find a full list of shortcuts.

5. Advanced Tips for Power Users

For users who want to maximize their efficiency with Viber, here are additional tips:

- **Combine Shortcuts**: For example, start a new chat (Ctrl + N), search for a contact (Ctrl + F), and quickly begin a call (Ctrl + Shift + C).

- **Use External Tools**: Tools like Stream Deck or macro-enabled keyboards can automate complex sequences of shortcuts for Viber.

- **Customize Shortcuts**: In some cases, you may be able to modify shortcut settings through your operating system for enhanced personalization.

- **Pair with Productivity Software**: Use Viber shortcuts alongside productivity apps like Trello or Google Calendar for seamless task management and communication.

6. Frequently Asked Questions About Viber Shortcuts

Q: Do keyboard shortcuts work on both Windows and macOS? A: Most shortcuts are universal; however, some may vary slightly between Windows and macOS. For example, replace "Ctrl" with "Cmd" on macOS.

Q: Can I customize shortcuts in Viber? A: As of now, Viber does not allow custom shortcut creation. You must use the default shortcuts provided by the app.

Q: Are there keyboard shortcuts for mobile versions of Viber? A: Keyboard shortcuts are only available for desktop versions of Viber. Mobile users can rely on touch gestures for navigation.

7. Conclusion

Keyboard shortcuts are a game-changer for anyone using Viber, whether casually or professionally. By mastering these shortcuts, you'll navigate through Viber faster, communicate more effectively, and enjoy a more streamlined experience overall. Take some time to practice these shortcuts, and you'll soon find that they save you valuable time in your daily communication tasks.

B. Glossary of Common Viber Terms

To help you navigate and make the most of your Viber experience, here is a comprehensive glossary of common terms used in the app. This section will serve as your quick reference guide to understanding Viber's features, functions, and technical jargon.

1. Account

Your personal profile on Viber that includes your name, phone number, profile picture, and settings. This account is tied to your phone number and serves as your identity on the app.

2. Archive Chat

A feature that allows you to hide conversations from your main chat list without deleting them. Archived chats can be accessed later and are particularly useful for organizing conversations.

3. Block

A privacy feature that allows you to prevent specific users from contacting you. When you block someone, they will not be able to message, call, or see your online status.

4. Bot

Automated accounts on Viber designed to provide information, entertainment, or services. Bots can be used for customer support, updates, games, and more.

5. Broadcast List

A way to send a single message to multiple contacts at once without creating a group chat. Recipients see the message as an individual chat, not part of a group.

6. Chat Background

The customizable wallpaper or background image for your conversations. You can choose from Viber's default designs or upload your own image.

7. Community

A group feature that allows large numbers of people to join and communicate in one space. Communities support an unlimited number of members and can include features like polls, announcements, and more.

8. Contact Sync

A feature that syncs your phone's contact list with Viber to identify which of your contacts are also using the app. It makes connecting with friends and family seamless.

9. Delete for Everyone

An option that allows you to delete a message you sent from both your chat and the recipient's chat. This feature is useful for correcting mistakes or removing messages sent in error.

10. Disappearing Messages

Messages that automatically delete after a set period. You can enable this feature in specific chats for enhanced privacy.

11. End-to-End Encryption

A security feature that ensures only the sender and recipient can read or listen to the messages and calls. Not even Viber can access your encrypted communications.

12. Group Chat

A conversation involving multiple participants. Group chats are ideal for families, friends, or teams who want to stay connected and share information.

13. Hidden Chats

A privacy feature that allows you to hide specific conversations from your main chat list. Hidden chats can be accessed with a PIN code for added security.

14. Invite

An option to send an invitation to your contacts to join Viber. You can invite people via text message, email, or social media.

15. Last Seen

A status indicator that shows the last time a user was active on Viber. You can control the visibility of your "last seen" status in your privacy settings.

16. Message Reaction

A feature that allows you to respond to a message with an emoji. This is a quick way to express emotions without sending a new message.

17. Notifications

Alerts that inform you of new messages, calls, or updates from Viber. Notifications can be customized or muted based on your preferences.

18. PIN Lock

A security feature that protects your hidden chats. Only users with the correct PIN can access these conversations.

19. Polls

A tool available in group chats and communities that lets you create questions with multiple answer options. Polls are useful for gathering opinions or making decisions as a group.

20. QR Code

A scannable code that allows you to quickly connect with another user or join a community. QR codes eliminate the need to share phone numbers.

21. Read Receipts

Indicators that show whether your message has been read by the recipient. Two checkmarks mean the message is delivered, and a colored checkmark means it has been read.

22. Secret Chat

A type of chat with enhanced privacy features, including disappearing messages and a ban on forwarding messages. Secret chats also prevent screenshots in certain devices.

23. Share Location

A feature that allows you to share your real-time location with another user. It's useful for coordinating meetups or letting someone know where you are.

24. Shortcut

A custom-created icon for specific Viber chats or groups that you can place on your phone's home screen for quick access.

25. Sticker

Graphics and illustrations used to express emotions or ideas in a conversation. Viber offers free and premium sticker packs, and you can even create your own.

26. Unsend Message

A feature that allows you to delete a sent message from your chat and the recipient's chat. Similar to "Delete for Everyone."

27. Viber Desktop

The desktop version of Viber that syncs with your mobile account. It allows you to send messages and make calls from your computer.

28. Viber Out

A paid service that allows you to make calls to landlines and non-Viber users at low rates. Ideal for international calling.

29. Video Call

A feature that enables face-to-face communication with other Viber users. Video calls can be made in both one-on-one and group settings.

30. Voice Message

An audio recording sent as a message. Voice messages are convenient for sharing longer thoughts or updates when typing isn't practical.

31. VoIP (Voice over Internet Protocol)

The technology that powers Viber calls, allowing voice and video communication over the internet instead of traditional phone lines.

32. Welcome Message

A customizable message sent automatically to new members who join a community. This is useful for setting expectations or sharing community guidelines.

33. Widget

A tool that allows you to access certain Viber features, such as recent chats or missed calls, directly from your phone's home screen.

34. Zero-Rate Plans

Special plans offered by some mobile operators that allow you to use Viber without consuming your data allowance.

35. Admin Rights

Special privileges granted to certain users in group chats or communities, allowing them to manage members, control settings, approve new participants, or moderate content.

36. Auto-Download

A setting that automatically downloads media files like photos, videos, and documents sent in chats. You can customize this feature to save data by enabling it only on Wi-Fi.

37. Broadcast Message

A one-way communication tool where admins in communities or group chats can send updates or announcements to all members. Unlike regular messages, replies are often disabled.

38. Chat Extensions

Built-in tools or integrations that allow users to perform actions directly within chats. Examples include searching for GIFs, playing music, or sharing links without leaving the app.

39. Cloud Backup

A feature that enables users to save their chat history and media files to a cloud storage service like Google Drive. This ensures data recovery when switching devices or reinstalling Viber.

40. Contact Status

An indicator that shows the current availability of your contacts, such as "Online," "Last Seen," or "Offline." This helps users know the best time to reach out.

41. Custom Sticker Packs

Personalized collections of stickers created by users. You can design your own sticker pack through Viber's sticker creation tool to add a unique touch to your conversations.

42. Dark Mode

A visual theme option that uses darker colors to reduce eye strain, save battery life on OLED screens, and enhance the user experience in low-light environments.

43. Default Chat Settings

Pre-set configurations for all new chats, such as default notification tones, media auto-download rules, and privacy preferences.

44. Discover Tab

A section in Viber where users can explore communities, official accounts, bots, and services for entertainment, news, and practical tools.

45. End Call Notification

An alert that informs you when a call has been disconnected, whether intentionally or due to technical issues. This helps ensure communication continuity.

46. File Sharing

A feature that allows you to send and receive documents, PDFs, presentations, and other file types directly through Viber chats, making it a handy tool for work or education.

47. Forwarding Limit

A restriction on how many times a message can be forwarded to reduce spam and misinformation. This reflects Viber's commitment to ethical communication.

48. Gif Search

An integrated tool that lets users search for and send animated GIFs to make conversations more expressive and entertaining.

49. Group Permissions

Customizable rules set by group admins that control what members can do, such as posting messages, sending media, or inviting others.

50. Link Preview

A feature that displays a snippet of a webpage when you share a URL in a chat. This includes the page title, description, and a thumbnail image for context.

51. Mark as Unread

A tool that allows users to mark a conversation as unread, serving as a reminder to revisit the chat later.

52. Mention

A feature that highlights a specific person in a group chat by tagging them with "@" followed by their name. This ensures they receive a notification even in busy conversations.

53. Message Pinning

The ability to pin a specific message at the top of a group chat or community for easy reference. This is often used for announcements or important updates.

54. Muting Chats

A setting that silences notifications for specific chats or groups for a designated time period. You can still view messages but won't be disturbed by alerts.

55. One-Tap Reply

A quick reply feature that allows you to respond to a specific message with a single tap. It's perfect for streamlined communication in busy chats.

56. Online Status

A visibility feature that shows whether you are currently active on Viber. You can choose to hide your online status for greater privacy.

57. Public Chat

A type of group or community designed for open participation, where anyone can join and view the messages without prior approval.

58. Reaction History

A log that shows all reactions to a specific message in a chat. This is particularly useful for group chats and communities where multiple users interact.

59. Smart Notifications

A feature that consolidates multiple notifications from the same chat into one alert, reducing interruptions while keeping you informed.

60. Spam Filtering

A security measure that automatically detects and filters out spam messages or suspicious links to protect users from scams and phishing.

61. Typing Indicator

An animation that appears in a chat when the other person is typing. This enhances real-time communication and sets expectations for replies.

62. Two-Step Verification

An added layer of security that requires a PIN code and email confirmation to protect your Viber account from unauthorized access.

63. Video Messages

Short video clips recorded and sent directly within chats. These are similar to voice messages but include visual content for added context.

64. Viber Stickers Market

A store where users can browse and purchase premium sticker packs to personalize their chats. Free stickers are also available.

65. Viber Out Credit

The prepaid balance used to make calls to non-Viber users or landlines through Viber Out. You can purchase credits directly in the app.

66. Voicemail

A feature that records messages when you miss a call on Viber. These recordings can be played back later at your convenience.

How to Use This Glossary

This glossary is designed to help you understand the terms and features that make Viber a powerful communication tool. Bookmark this section for easy access whenever you encounter a term you're unfamiliar with. By mastering these terms, you'll unlock the full potential of Viber and enhance your experience with the app.

Acknowledgments

First and foremost, I want to express my heartfelt gratitude to you, the reader, for choosing to purchase this book. Your time, trust, and investment in this guide mean the world to me. It is your curiosity and dedication to learning that inspire the creation of resources like this one.

Thank you for allowing this book to accompany you on your journey to mastering Viber. Whether you are a first-time user or someone looking to unlock the app's full potential, I hope the pages of this book have provided you with valuable insights, practical tips, and the confidence to make the most of Viber's features.

To those who shared feedback, ideas, and encouragement along the way, your contributions were instrumental in shaping this book. A special thanks to friends, family, and colleagues who offered their support during the writing process.

Finally, this book would not have been possible without the amazing community of Viber users worldwide. Your passion for connecting, communicating, and building meaningful relationships is what makes platforms like Viber so special.

If this book has made your Viber experience easier, more enjoyable, or more productive, I would love to hear from you! Please don't hesitate to share your thoughts, feedback, or success stories.

Once again, thank you for reading, and happy messaging!

Warm regards,